PROJECT MANAGEMENT

An Organizational Psychology Perspective

Second Edition

PROJECT MANAGEMENT

An Organizational Psychology Perspective

Second Edition

Thomas A. Browdy
Alberts-Adams, LLC
St. Louis, Missouri

This publication is design to be used with educational opportunities in project management. This book in not provided to recommend professional opinion nor guarantee results.

Browdy, Thomas A., 1947 -
© 2009 Thomas A. Browdy.

To my children, Sarah and Jacob

PREFACE

Project Management

This book is being written to fulfill my desire to document what I've learned teaching the subject for over 15 years mostly to Information Technology professionals through training courses and graduate level courses in Information Management at Washington University in St. Louis. After having read the serious, and the not so serious literature concerning this subject, I've been convinced there is a great deal missing in bringing the expertise of great project managers to others. I've encountered many of these great project managers over the years by on-site investigations and consulting, in training programs, and in graduate courses. While the literature does an adequate job of identifying the importance of these people and their characteristics, there is a lack of information on how they do what they do. Knowledge is important, but also having the ability to put that knowledge to use is especially important in the area of project management. After all, it is all about getting something done. If there ever was a characteristic of a good project manager, it is the ability to "get things done".

So venture once again within this book through the three things that make education valuable – knowledge, skill, and an ability to think about it (frameworks of understanding).

Preface to Second Edition

There's more than one reason a second edition of this book is necessary but the predominant one is the lack of clarity in the first edition. Almost the day after the first edition was published I knew it was not all it should be. Further explanation seemed to be needed in many parts to grasp major points, let alone the more subtle ones. Since the book was primarily used in education and training settings these explanations were usually forthcoming and the book's weakness ignored. With this new edition I would like the reader to conclude after reading a chapter "I see", rather than "I think I get it, but…"

It's my humble belief that the subject is not complex, but without supporting discussion the first edition often made it appear that way. I submit that project management education is to a large part about providing frameworks for the knowledge that most people already have (especially since life is filled with projects). Everyone can solve problems – it's knowing how you've solved them that provides insight for the next time. So this book is mostly about frameworks and how they can be used to provide insight, while initiating the serious student to a mastery track. This mastery track melds the practice of project management with its learning – doing is learning provided you know how "to do" and how "to learn".

This melding of practice and learning I know to be true because I've seen it in action. It's evident from those who've mastered the approach offered in this book, as well as to those who nod their heads when they see that what they've been doing has a framework that increases their understanding and integrates their knowledge into a more complete picture.

Knowledge about how things work is important, but understanding why they work the way they do is even more important. Continual practice leads to increased understanding and eventually to the wisdom of knowing when to do what – wisdom integrates knowledge into practice. Encountering wisdom usually means encountering a master, and finding the road of mastery is what this book is about.

Tom Browdy

Table of Contents

Table of Contents

PART ONE

Introduction

This book is written for both the new and experienced project manager. The main premise of this work is to consider each person as an experienced project manager, but missing a formalism (framework) on how to plan and carry out a successful project. Sections throughout the book labeled "projects of life" are everyday experiences viewed as projects (i.e. *getting to work* as a project). Since life is filled with projects what's missing is a way to organize these experiences in a framework that can be refined and reused. The book is laid out around the parametric analysis framework which organizes existing personal knowledge on projects.

While a good project manager finds a way to understand the project, and then adjust what has to be done based on that understanding; a master project manager finds a way to integrate the knowledge of every project into a personal skill set that can be used on future projects. Unfortunately the way to project management mastery is usually such a personal journey of learning that a common approach is nearly impossible. It's not unlike many professions that are founded on practice rather than just knowledge or position. If you can't manage a project you can't really be a project manager. It's like martial arts, music performance, medicine, law, and architecture. Knowledge is important, but putting it to use is key – it's not so much what you know, but how you can arrange your knowledge in a way that leads to effective performance. Some advanced knowledge only comes from performance and not study.

The parametric approach is a way to understand and integrate knowledge of what it takes to be an effective project manager. It provides a practice field for someone pursuing mastery. Mastery requires practice, and practicing with a real project is very risky and slows learning. It's like performing surgery for the first time on a patient without practicing how to make an incision. Practicing on the real thing can be disastrous. One can learn project specifics, but it's more important to understand them in a holistic/total way. Part one examines fundamental frameworks that will be relied on throughout the remaining chapters, part two includes primary/filtering parameters that will simplify the process of understanding, parts three, four, and five (chapters five through twelve) examine specific parameters that make up the concept of project management, and part six (chapters thirteen and fourteen) the process of conducting a parametric analysis.

The important learning is not the particulars of each parameter, but the overall approach of a parametric analysis. A parametric analysis reveals possibilities for what could be done to manage a project and serves to integrate present experiences of managing a project with past ones – builds advanced knowledge that leads to mastery.

Chapter 1

Fundamental Frameworks

Managing projects has not been the most successful endeavor in recent history. The number of project failures have been heralded publicly (Standish Group, 1995) and whispered across water coolers privately. Tools have been developed and deployed to aid in managing projects, but their contribution toward project success appears to be very questionable. Not that tools are unimportant, they are not *all*-important. Knowledge about project management has been available for many years. A scan of the bibliography of this book shows literature that dates back over 20 years. A way to both understand and actively manage projects is missing. Like many other conceptual notions projects are much easier to devise than they are to carry out. What's needed is: one, a way to organize the knowledge; two, a way to put it into practice; and three, reasons for why things work the way they do. This last item provides a deeper insight that will make the other two more useful in a variety of environments.

Yet, just as other professions have gone through changes, both with technology and improved processes, so project management also is in need of much improvement. It's not that we cannot manage a project to success, but that we are not sure from one project to the next if this will be possible. We lack perspective and insight. Getting these is not "Elementary, Dr. Watson", but comes with practice along with integrated personal knowledge. We need a framework to integrate this knowledge and insights about human behavior. Expecting to only gather this knowledge and insight from managing various projects is much like the expression: "Living in a cave does not make you a geologist" (Galdwell, 2007).

A look at great athletes shows how knowledge and insight (through practice and real life play) integrates into potential excellent performance. It's been claimed that Larry Bird, of Boston NBA Celtics basketball fame, could see the whole court at once and was constantly aware of everyone's location. This made him the master of the court and helped the Celtics achieve outstanding performance. Projects are more complicated than basketball; you can't manage this project like the last. It would be like playing basketball on the moon without practice. Even in basketball one team will require a different approach than another. The team in your project may be analogous to an Apollo space launch team, or like one of the gangs of New York. So, having and using a framework about projects and the people in them can prove very valuable.

Getting in the Game Of Project Management

Projects begin as a fantasy that obtain an aura of reality when formed into a plan. To our chagrin they remain elusive fantasies through most of their approval cycle, and then begin to accumulate characteristics that make them seem more real. They roll through committees, across desks for opinions, under signatures for stakeholders, and on lists for approval or denial. With all the up-front work said and done the project has become an interesting fiction or well-organized hope. To apply standard scientific or causal thinking to the project at this point is like trying to prove that a game of baseball is really a game. We would be better off making sure we knew the rules of baseball and how the game is usually played based on prevailing conditions. Three strikes and you're out can't be proven. If third base is open, no one is out, and your leadoff batter is up, you may want to try a squeeze bunt. You can't prove this is what you should do by causal reasoning, nor can you find it in the rules. It's circumstantial and depends on too many variables to be entirely predictive. If in the game Monopoly one of your opponents has a property that you need and you land on one she needs, you may want to buy it and initiate a trade. This is not in the rules, nor can you predict when such a strategy would be successful (it may depend on how much cash is available at that point in the game, along with how stubborn your opponent might be when facing a trade situation). These situations are more like what it takes to manage projects than refining a predictive detailed plan of action. We need a way to know the "game" of project management and then play it according to what rules there are and what wisdom may apply. This book aspires to teach the game, its rules and patterns, and how to play the game with a certain degree of wisdom, and eventually master it. As with Monopoly or chess, really good players can recognize certain patterns during the game and react appropriately. Good project managers recognize patterns that lend themselves to taking certain actions. When the next project comes along, those that know the game will be ready to play, those that don't will be crouched behind the photocopier upon the announcement "we have a new project". When you've mastered an approach to managing projects, you can begin each new project without much fear of being trampled by it, and with the exciting expectation that "the game's afoot", and you'll walk away from the effort with improved project management knowledge and/or insight.

Project Management Success: Limits on The Causal Approach

On a hot summer afternoon we four lads are headed for the swimming pool. A quick trip through the bathhouse, our trunks in place, we're ready for fun and games in the pool. As our enthusiasm takes over we *run* out of the bathhouse only to be whistled down by the lifeguard who shouts: "No running! Running on wet cement will cause you to slip, fall and hurt yourself". This is not unlike the idea expressed in a favorite Christmas movie: "You don't really want a BB gun; you'll shoot your eye out, kid".

These circumstances show that many people live as if causal relationships are true even though they know they're not. We all want to know what produces project success, and for many people this means discovering and executing the tasks that cause success. Success is produced but it isn't caused. Producing success requires knowing the conditions and options available under these conditions, and adjusting to changing conditions. Discovering the necessary and sufficient conditions that lead to project success is fruitless. The oft-touted conditions for project success are easy to accept and easy to remember, but represent a wrong way of thinking about projects. Some are listed in Figure 1.1.

> Management Support
> End User Involvement
> Formal Planning Process
> Change Control in Place
> Carefully Picked Team
> Authority Formally Bestowed

Conditions for Project Success
Figure 1.1

Examining the condition of *management support* will show how these simple answers are inappropriate. This condition is probably one of the most espoused reasons for project success/failure as any. It's usually provided as a post-hoc reason for project failure. If it failed it must be management's fault. Seldom is it used for project success. Success is attributed to the team or individuals who went the extra mile.

Actor-Observer Effect
Over attribute our own behavior to the situation factors rather than to personal characteristics.

Why would people attribute success/failure in such a way? Psychologically speaking it is a form of the actor-observer effect (over attributing our own behavior as being influenced by the situation), the fundamental attribution error (over attributing behavior of others to their personal characteristics), and the self-serving bias (over

Fundamental Attribution Error
Over attribute another person's behavior to his or her own personal characteristics rather than to situational factors.

Self-Serving Bias
Over attribute success to our own behavior and failure to situation factors.

attributing success of the outcome to personal efforts and over attributing failure to achieve the outcome to the circumstances). From the project manager's perspective management failed if the project failed (over attributing failure to a situational factor), the project team was successful if the project was successful (over attributing success to the "person"/project team rather than circumstances) (Fisk, 1984). Projects can be found for all possible attributions of success or failure due to management support or lack of support (see Figure 1.2).

		Management Support	
		YES	NO
Success	YES	A	B
	NO	C	D

Attributions for Management Support
Figure 1.2

Cells "C" and "B" are not null and present interesting cases. In cell "C" you can have management support and still not be successful. This means there are other possible things that may be needed to achieve success. Management support is not *sufficient*. In cell "B" we find success without management support. In this case management support is not *necessary*. This one seems counter-intuitive, yet if you think about what goes on in many high R&D environments the last thing you may want is management support. What you may want is management uninvolved. If this is management support then we may want to reconsider the word "support". The other conditions for project success fall into the same trap – they seem causal, but are neither necessary nor sufficient. Therefore the cause-effect reasoning that relies on necessary and sufficient conditions causing outcomes is an inappropriate way of thinking about managing projects. Another way of understanding projects is needed.

The non-causal relationship between actions and outcomes on a project irritates and at times confuses many logical/scientific reasoners. IF it happened there must be a logical/reasonable reason. However, some things that happen on a project defy reason. When confronted with failure, and subsequently ready to begin a new project, logical reasoners often post-hoc analyze what CAUSED the failure, and then add to their mental mindset the causal reasons for project failure. They misattribute the failure (e.g. to bad planning, when it was simply the CEO was angered at the project leader from the last project) and use the attribution to plan and sidestep failure in the next project. This mental set is organized incorrectly because it's based on the wrong premise. Most technical projects are managed by people who have learned to look at the world this way, and hence miss the value of an evolutionary understanding that comes from each project's success or failure. Project managers have to think broader

Lessons that have been espoused by good project mangers provide a clearer indication of how to produce success because they point to the circumstances that surround every project. There are at least six categories of lessons (leadership, communicating requirements, change management, task aspects, people emphasis, and communicating with stakeholders). *Leadership* encompasses all aspects required to manage, coordinate, sell, and cajole the project to a final successful conclusion. *Communicating requirements* category involves making sure the requirements of the project are stated as clearly as possible and there's agreement with major stakeholders about these requirements. *Change management* focuses on setting the environment up for change and actually facilitating and sometime advocating for a change as the project's major deliverable is ushered into its environment. *Task aspects* are a micro view of the necessities of the project – what needs to be done and who needs to do it. *People emphasis* focuses on the individual and collective motivations and behaviors of the people in and around the project. *Communicating with stakeholders* is more than just making sure the requirements are clear. Stakeholder communication is an ongoing effort so they will maintain their support throughout the projects duration (Browdy, 2007).

Frameworks for Understanding and Managing Projects

Aunt Genny is an example of the reasonable philosophical argument: *If there is one way to describe something, there's also another* (Ossorio, 1981). Everybody had their opinion of my Aunt Genny. Some thought she was harsh and too bossy because she used to tell my Uncle Curley (that's what she called him) what to do from one moment to the next. Others thought she was a "card". Good for a laugh and able to reach into the everyday circumstances of life and see something interesting. I can still remember how she used to keep her cigarettes in a prominent place in the middle of her body when wearing a summer low cut top. She was sometimes privately denigrated because she lacked significant education. I found this endearing and made her even more real and unencumbered. My favorite expression of hers, secretly written down just after she spoke, is: "Them ain't ducks, thems dears". Just as everyone had their opinion of Aunt Genny, there are many ways to understand and provide insight into managing projects. Although you are welcome to disagree, the following five ways to understand projects are very beneficial.

1. The systems approach
2. The three worlds
3. Parametric analysis
4. Individual differences (hemispheric specialization)
5. Community of Practice approach

These are discussed briefly below. Just as with Aunt Genny, you're welcome to form your own opinion of each, however these can stand up to considerable scrutiny.

Systems Approach

Complicated items hung together in unpredictable and changing ways have been described using systems theory (Boulding, 1956; L. von Bertalanffy, 1951; Churchman, 1968; Senge, 1990). Systems thinking about a particular system points us toward looking for its containing system and its existing and emergent properties. This approach is not caught up in causal thinking that examines details of the system by breaking it into its elemental parts looking for absolute conditional relationships. A project is not a static entity waiting for conditions that will yield success. The project itself is being remolded by the system(s), of which it is a part, where each part has its own purpose. If one of these systems is to please management, and management is pleased when supportive, then management support should tip the scale toward success. The management support imperative is caught both in the organizational cultural expectations as well as in personal desires/expectations of individual managers. Such success conditions are not the same for all projects, and can't be concluded as a general condition for success.

System thinking examines the containing set of systems that matter. These containing systems, or worlds, do not represent a set of cause-effect conditions for success, but provide an interpretation so that the efficacy of doing one thing over another can be better understood. These containing systems for a project will be addressed as parameters below.

The Worlds of Project Management

There are always three worlds that can be considered. These are the world of *machines*, the world of *people*, and the world of *numbers* (Putman, 1988). So as not to confuse the world of numbers with just accounting, the word *strategic* will be used. Strategic should suggest an overall importance to the bottom-line, a market driven mentality, a matter of enterprise survival, etc. (see Figure 1.3). Interpreting projects from these three worlds can provide

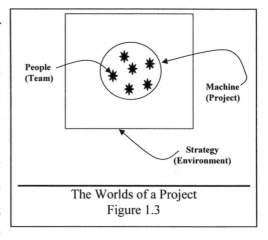

The Worlds of a Project
Figure 1.3

reasons why some projects should be managed one way and other projects another. All three worlds should be considered for every project but usually there is a dominant one which is most useful for prioritizing when to do what. Back to a game analogy, it's like playing three different games each with their own set of rules. Important items in each world are represented by parameters, and using these parameters will organize the abundant knowledge about project management.

The three worlds provide a way to organize all the aspects of a project. The world of *people* is predominantly about the project team itself. Considerations include team formation, leadership of the team, and motivational approaches. There are clearly *people* relationships between team members and those outside the project team that may warrant a people worldview, but outside team relationships often are about the business impact of the project and could be best understood from a *strategic* worldview. The *strategic* world is about environmental, or suprasystem, considerations for the project. These considerations include stakeholders representing the eventual business impact, the characteristics of the enterprise, and the dynamics of change to the environment itself.

The *machine* world viewpoint is a way the project, as a particular kind of work can be interpreted. Project, in this sense, includes the basic ingredients of a project, formal planning, formal control, as well as the problem orientation taken to produce the final deliverable.

Parametric Approach

A complex concept, such as managing a project, can be acted upon by dividing each world into its constituent parts, or parameters, and examining how the pieces interact. These pieces have a relationship with one another but the relationships change when the world of understanding changes. Systems thinking tells us to look for these relationships, or interactions, and not be concerned with breaking them down into indivisible elements or units of analysis (reductionism) (Ackoff, 1981). Also, it doesn't take too many elements to make memorizing every combination impossible. A parametric approach provides access to the possible interactions, and a way to think about them. This is what good project managers do, they don't look for cookbook answers but for the real issues that must be faced and dealt with by interpreting the worlds as they have come to know them. It's like mastering anything, like chess, before long you get to recognize patterns of interaction and make moves based on an overall pattern rather than particular pieces. The parametric approach provides a way to construct patterns as they unfold and make the right moves. With experience, some patterns will become more immediately evident leading to timely actions on the part of the project manager.

---

1. Breaks the space into manageable chunks

2. Provides all the possible combinations

3. Highlights the interactive nature of parameters

4. Provides a learnable framework that is useful for interpretation

Benefits of a Parametric Analysis

Figure 1.4

Learning the parameters and their interactions is a mastery step. Just as Gladwell reports in his book *Blink*, when masters view something they see more than what is plainly obvious. They "time slice" the whole into an immediate discernable sense of what there really is and what it means. For project managers this is reading the whole project from a few critical parameters. The parametric approach will be used to open the door to mastery of project management.

Organizing the three worlds with a set of parameters in each provides clear distinctions that assist any project manager in interpreting entire projects. The sets of parameters provided in this book are gleaned from the literature on project management, general management, and interactions with hundreds of successful project managers. The sets are not necessarily complete, so adding, or even deleting, parameters may be useful as one gains experience both as a project manager and at using this overall technique. The relationship of parameters within each of the three worlds is shown in Figures 1.5 and 1.6.

Parameters in each of the three worlds, while having relationships to one another, just as I have a relationship with my car, fundamentally remain in their own worlds. Actions taken, as represented by a particular parameter, will result in fairly predictable results, but may have surprising results in the other worlds unless they are examined from the particular world's point of view. If I step on the accelerator of my car, the car will predictably go faster (unless something goes wrong). But when the car accelerates I may get a "rush" or excited as a person. Explaining this "rush" from the world of *machines* would be possible but not all that useful. Hence it's informative to examine parameters from different world viewpoints.

If a people result is needed, then it's best to examine the relationship from the *people* world. If I want a bigger "rush" from my relationship with the car, a people world result, I may want to increase the acceleration. There are so many more possibilities that will be missed if the relationship is examined from the *machine* world. The *machine* world may suggest "sooping up" the engine, getting a high-octane fuel, etc. The people world may suggest rolling all the windows down, driving a convertible, and having someone special with me for example.

While this example may seem to provide little insight into managing a project, consider motivating a team. From the world of *people* there are many opportunities, but from the *machine* world more pay may be a top suggestion since there is an apparent mechanistic relationship between pay and performance (Locke, 1981). From the world of people, you may get more motivated behavior out of each team member if you get rid of the non-performer everyone feels they're carrying on their backs (see Chapter 11).

Each parameter has a set of values associated with it. These values represent a state of reality for the parameter. For instance, how a *team* is structured has four values one of which is the *specialty* team. Some parameters have values that may be limited to subjective interpretation such as *low, medium*, or *high* (see the planning parameter). For instance, a project may not have a clear leader; leader is one of the values of the *basics* parameter (chapter 2).

Figures 1.5 and 1.6 show the sixteen parameters, identifies them as primary or secondary, depicts the values they can take on, and the chapters that cover each.

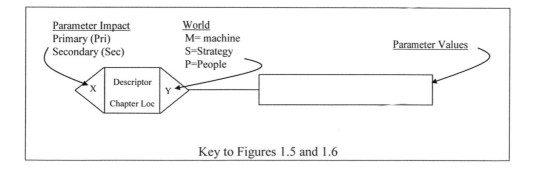

Key to Figures 1.5 and 1.6

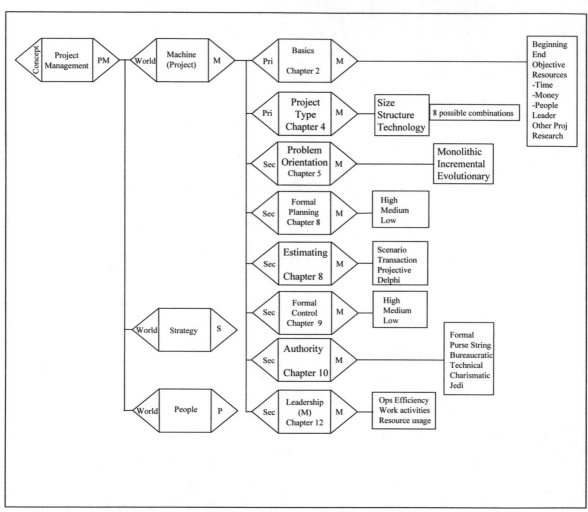

Parameters Organization by Worlds - Machine
Figure 1.5

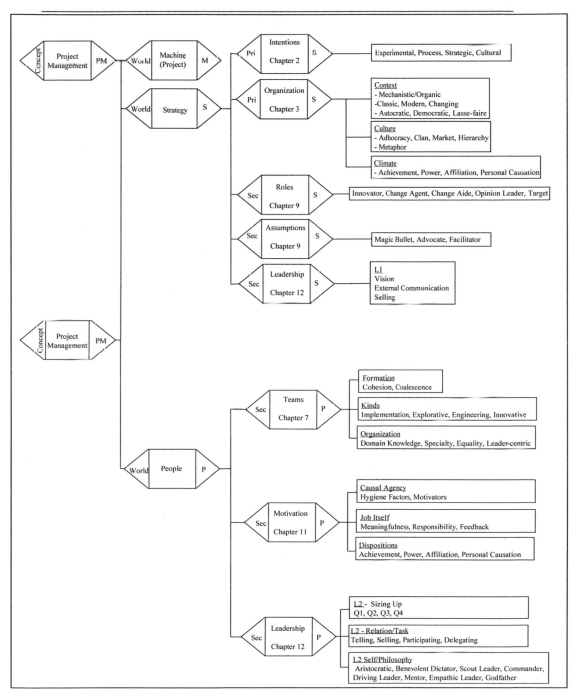

Parameters Organization by Worlds – Strategy and People
Figure 1.6

Additional parameters can be accommodated within the structure (or deleted) depending upon the context. Discovering the most important parameters is the result of a parametric analysis described later. Also other analyses can be useful for managing projects. Parametric analyses have been developed for *Change Management*, and for *The Person* (Browdy, 2007).

Preferred Ways of Behaviors: Individual Differences

If you ask people familiar with project work, most will have little trouble listing activities in which successful project managers engage. However, they aren't as confident about knowing when or which of these activities should take place, how exactly they should be performed, and at what level of effort (see Figure 1.7). There are too many to consider, so behaviors that are preferred, but not necessarily needed, will usually get the bulk of attention by the project manager. If you're relatively accomplished at something (usually because it's been your preferred way of managing a project) you may find yourself groping at times because you need to do something that is not one of your preferences. Many project mangers fall victim to the "We've always done it that way" mentality. It's like the old joke: "Why are you looking for your keys under this light, I thought you lost them over there? Because the light's better over here."

Activities	Left/Right
Form a plan	L
Motivate staff	R
Communicate with users	R
Talk with management	R
Report progress	R
Keep the project on target	R/L
Develop schedule	L
Estimate task durations	L
Assign resources	L
Acquire resources	R/L
Conduct walk-thrus	L
Know the problem	L
Form coalitions	R
Present results	L/R
Apply change control	L
Report on milestones	L
Establish milestones	L

Success Activities
Figure 1.7

What you want to do to be successful on a project may not be what you need to do. Some people will prefer certain activities from the list, while other people will prefer other activities. Brain hemispheric specialization is one way to look at individual differences and spot preferences. Much experimental evidence and assessment instruments attest to the differences between people who prefer one side of their brain more than the other. Some people are more right brained, others more left. Right-brain people see the whole (versus parts), assimilate quickly, and deal with emergent properties of the situation relatively easily. They see the forest but may miss the trees. Left-brained people are detail oriented, see causal relationship relatively easily, and are usually very rational. They miss the forest for the trees. There is evidence that points to left-brained people being good at planning, and right-brained good at managing (Mintzberg, 1976). The left-brained is logical and cause-effect oriented, while the right-brained handles surprises and deals with the world holistic. (See Figures 1.7 and 1.8)

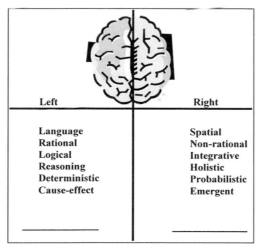

Hemispheric Specialization
Figure 1.8

Not all activities need to be carried out for every project, and some are more important than others. Activities actually performed on projects are a combination of what the project calls for, and what individual preferences are at play. See Appendix A for a short self-assessment on hemispheric dominance. By using the assessment instrument you will be able to see what project activities you may need to spend extra effort performing.

If the project manager only does what seems easiest and natural, then a critical activity for achieving project success may be missed. Performing a non-dominant activity is like writing with your non-dominant hand. It can be done, but it takes extra effort and attention. The point is to reduce the preference bias. You may prefer certain activities to others, but acting on these preferences because they feel right at the time may be a result of just preference rather than what would be best.

Mastery and Project Management

While in the first part of a short career in the Air Force my goal was to get through basic electronics training without over-expending myself. As a young man there were plenty of things to do other than spend a lot of mental, emotional, or physical energy in electronics training. Do my time and get on with the next assignment. This was both socially acceptable to my buddies, and really matched my well-developed skill for doing as little work as possible. My goal was to get done. Then it happened. I flunked one set of the series that was required. An officer responsible for training the troops counseled me in ways mom may have found offensive. I was told I'd be assigned to the slower learning group, offered the "option" of study hall, and told to get it in gear or I'd be cooking (read: pulling permanent KP) in Vietnam. This was 1966. Goals are pipedreams without working components. Okay, that goal of just getting through was not going to work. I wasn't sure what the new goal should be, so devotion to really learning the stuff took over. Having lucked onto a new devotion, coupled with the idea that my behavior had to change if I wanted a different outcome, personal achievement resulted. I received commendations in each of the remaining sets of training classes. I may not have been able to recognize the new goal, but I knew I was on a new path. One of my mentors along this path related to me that it isn't how smart you are but how persistently hard you try. This was my initiation to a road of mastery for learning that stayed with me throughout my Air Force

> Goals may be okay but once you decide on a journey they become secondary.

and university career. Without it, I may have ended up flipping hamburgers -- although becoming a master chef is a worthy pursuit.

Mastery is a path not a goal. It's a step function where each step or plateau provides opportunity to practice, and eventually be rewarded with a higher level of achievement. Mastery requires the trait of delayed gratification. The steps of practice are repetitive, not immediately rewarding, nor equally accomplished within the same timeframe for every individual (see Figure 1.9).

Mastering project management means commitment: Getting on the path and not just deciding on the goals. It requires dedication and it means surrender: Thinking good enough is not good enough. George Leonard in his little book on *Mastery* outlines five keys:

1. Instruction: You need a teacher.
2. Practice: Something separated from the rest of your life.
3. Surrender: To your teacher, to the discipline, away from personal dignity.
4. Intentionality: See a vision of what is to be accomplished.
5. Edge: Test the edges in search of a larger/greater outcome.
(Leonard, 1992)

Leonard applies what he had learned in martial arts to almost every pursuit of life. His evidence to support mastery in all we do is sparse and he could be severely criticized for over-generalization, but he does shed light on what it takes to be a real master. Mastery is clearly not something that one acquires in a three-day training session, or in a two week training boot camp designed to pass a test.

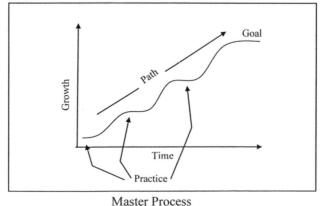

Master Process
Figure 1.9

Mastery Through Structure

Another approach at mastery is to put it into a context that outlines the steps -- for the trades it is apprentice, journeyman, and master. Each of these is a plateau that requires continuing commitment, dedication, and surrender. The apprentice works under a skilled professional in order to learn an art, craft, or trade and become qualified in it. A journeyman is a qualified artisan that has completed an apprenticeship and is fully trained and qualified but still works under guidance. He/she is a competent and reliable performer without being brilliant or outstanding. A master is highly skilled in a trade or craft and is qualified to teach apprentices. Achieving the mastery level means one goes beyond introductory or minimum competence levels.

Recognizing Mastery

The idea of mastery fits with a variety of areas – sports, martial arts, games, medicine, and music to name a few. Recognition may come in a variety of ways. The Masters' golf tournament invites people who have proven themselves by standings and winnings. Some martial arts recognize mastery by the black belt. Games also have their mastery level. Chess masters are clearly different than the average chess player. A chess master is recognized by a point system requiring accumulation over a period of time, which necessitates actually playing the game. You can't just read about chess and pass a test to be a master - you have to perform.

Mastery is a journey to new plateaus not a one-time achievement, its belief in future plateaus that are now possible. New plateaus are possible by practice within the current plateau. Good enough is not good enough. Tiger Woods still practices and Mickey Mantle took batting practice. One of the greatest violinists of all time, Itzhak Perlman, said "I am playing the violin, that's all I know, nothing else, no education, no nothing. *You just practice every day*." Chess players reach a new plateau when they can visualize the whole board and not just the individual pieces. They are looking for patterns that give insight into the next and future possible moves.

Experienced professionals, such as nurses, experience plateaus of practice (Benner, 2001). They need to grow in the ability to become an expert in their chosen profession. It starts with the level of *novice* where the professional only knows context-free attributes of what to do (e.g. take their temperature and blood pressure) and in Dreyfus' framework of professional growth proceeds to *expert maturing*. The *advanced beginner* sees global aspects from past experiences and is able to make quicker decisions. The *competent* professional sees not only what is immediate but long term repercussions of an action or treatment. The *proficient* professional sees holistically, and is able to use maxims to gain insight into problems. The professional sees and judges each case based on loose collections of ideas that can be applied to see inductively what is the case. The *expert* professional takes disjointed ideas and impressions and reacts in smooth treatment and decision making for an eventual positive outcome (Dreyfus, 1981) (see Table 1-1).

	Level	Description	Elapsed Timeframe
Apprentice	Novice	Works on measurable context free attributes (has only theory as a guide)	6 months
Apprentice	Advanced Beginner	Overall global aspects are identified by prior experience (guidelines)	1-2 years
Journeyman	Competent	Sees long range goals and repercussions. Acts within a broader boundary.	2-3 years
Journeyman	Proficient	Thinks and see holistically, uses maxims. The individual situation speaks of itself (inductive)	5 years
Master	Expert	Not analytic principles (rules, guidelines, maxims). Goes from jerky actions to smooth.	5+ years
Master	Expert Maturing	Continuing growth and seeing new ways. Gains insight into the practice itself.	5+ years

Professional Elements of Mastery
Table 1-1

The general aspects, of expert/skilled performance, moves from reliance on abstract principles to use of concrete experiences as paradigms. An expert can move to a complete holistic understanding where only parts are evident. They can get it all by seeing just some of its pieces. Also, the professional reaching the expert level moves from detached observation to active performance. Some experts get into the performance so much that they experience a kind of flow that separates them from the confines of the present experience. The performance, by an improving professional, moves from jagged to smooth, from the left side of the brain dealing with details, to the right side that deals with holistic issues and intuitive interpretations.

Practical knowledge, particularly at the expert level, is best studied holistically within its containing context of understanding not separated from it. When an expert is embedded within the full context of their performance what happens is often unexplainable by the expert alone – they know more than they can tell. Some firemen experience this in instances where they know when to escape a burning building just before it falls (Schon, 1987).

A Taxonomy of Learning

One of the most famous and used ways to understand learning is from Benjamin Bloom. In Bloom's taxonomy of learning (Bloom, 1956) one might proceed to a mastery level, where the top category, *evaluation*, is a sign of mastery. In this approach the student gets more proficient in the topic by acquiring the skill to know, comprehend, apply, analyze, synthesize, and then evaluate.

Knowledge is a static learning outcome. Do I know what, when, who? Having the knowledge means being able to recall it and know in general to what domain of understanding it belongs. The significance of the knowledge is not well understood. Simply knowing Project Management Institute's (PMI®) Project Management Body of Knowledge (PMBOK) will not make one a good project manager. *Comprehension* requires an interpretation of the knowledge. At this level one can discuss the knowledge in a context and explain its relevancy. *Application* of knowledge is being able to make the knowledge useful in solving problems. *Analysis* means taking a problem and dividing it into its component parts to see what knowledge is required to understand the problem in more detail. *Synthesis* requires creativity to combine ideas and design alternative solutions. *Evaluation* is being able to look at a whole problem and see the possible explanations for its current and future state. It could be judging the outcome based on values, competencies, or various perspectives. Mastery can be achieved by proceeding up this taxonomy (see Table 1-2).

A more recent usage of Bloom's taxonomy (2001) is represented as a four tiered approach. The approach has as tier one *remembering*, two *understanding*, three *applying*, and four shared by *analyzing, evaluating* and *creating*.

	Category	Definition	Question words	Example
Apprentice	Knowledge	Information that can be memorized and recalled	Who, what, when, where, list	What are the eight ingredients of a project?
Apprentice	Comprehension	Interpreting and paraphrasing knowledge	Restate, discuss, describe	Discuss the advantages of a project member who is high in need for achievement.
Journeyman	Application	Problem solving and applying information	Interpret, apply, use	Describe the team structure that would accommodate a team whose members come and go relatively quickly.
Journeyman	Analysis	Subdivide into component parts, determining motives	Compare, contrast, examine	Examine the critical success factors of the *Junk Yard Dog* project.
Master	Synthesis	Creativity by combining ideas	Compose, develop, construct, design	Develop a complete plan for project *X*.
Master	Evaluation	Judgment, making value decisions	Judge, appraise, evaluate, assess	Assess the likely outcome of project *X*.

Bloom's Taxonomy
Table 1-2

Community of Practice (CoP)

There are a variety of paths one can take to achieve mastery in project management. In fact there are so many that almost any initiation into the area can yield a mastery result. This grand scheme is called the school of hard knocks. You learn or fail to become a master by managing projects. Survival rate is not high for this approach. There is help along the way through education and, to some degree, standards set by individual enterprises or through formal groups that may be pursing a common set of knowledge, such as the Project Management Institute (PMI®). While knowledge and standards may be well articulated, one cannot become a master project manager by knowing them. You actually have to be able to perform project management just like a chess master has to play.

In order to learn performance you need to actually be in the game in some way. Practice helps increase game performance, but practice for project managers means learning to manage a project without really managing a project. There are several ways to do this. Simulation of a project is one, a parametric analysis another, evaluating other projects a third (*evaluation* being Bloom's highest level of learning), and case study analysis.

A group is needed for practicing project management in order to achieve the expert/mastery level. The group needs a guide, or teacher, and ways to communicate that permits the teacher/master/expert to share their knowledge with the novices and less capable (e.g. the medical doctor making rounds with medical students). Shared practical knowledge is possible by identifying key lessons (maxims, tenets) of project management learned by the experts from their practice. Some of these can be caught, and subsequently taught, in a formal framework but most key lessons come from such a rich context that generalized frameworks or limited simulations will not reveal them. This is where a Community of Practice (CoP) can be helpful.

A CoP is focused on learning from a group in such a way that the group can judge the mastery level of achievement of its participants. A CoP is informally bound together by shared expertise and passion for joint performance. While the CoP is informal it's possible to be deliberate in formation where individuals are already connected in some way toward the pursuit of a collective goal. CoPs have been formed for consultants in strategic marketing, managers in charge of processing in a large bank, and safety boards to name a few. According to Etienne Wenger, formulator of the CoP idea, these CoPs can generate strategy, solve complex problems, generate new lines of business, and develop professional skills. Establishing a CoP is one way to achieve mastery in project management (Wenger, 2006).

A CoP is a way to transform best practices from documented observations into performance. The CoP is an on-going endeavor that provides learning at various levels and generates identity to what it means for participants/community members to be a part of the practice, in our case, what it means to be a project management master.

The key to learning within the CoP is the ability to negotiate meaning in and around performance. Negotiation occurs when practices are viewed as a duality. They have the qualities of reification and participation. Reification is the embodiment of the practice. The constitution is the reification of citizenship. Reification brings the reality of

practice into a place that is tangible and can be connected logically with other parts –
books on chess are reifications of the actual game. Participation is doing what the
practice is, while reification codifies or manifests the practice in devices such as
frameworks, models, or descriptive patterns. When these devices don't catch the practice,
negotiation should potentially occur, producing new meanings. A key lesson learned for
project managers is not to let stakeholders be surprised. How do you do this? It's both a
list of what to do/not do (reification), and exercising what is on the list (participation).
When the CoP interacts over time toward the goal with passion for producing master
project managers not only will the result be master project managers but a way to evolve
the profession so that new levels of mastery can be achieved. New lessons will be
revealed.

The idea of a CoP can be applied to a particular project team/group, rather than a
way to achieve mastery of the overall concept. Plans and planning a particular project
involves the notions of participation and reification. Planning is participating, but the plan
is reification. Dwight D. Eisenhower said: "I have always found that plans are useless,
but planning is indispensable." He saw the importance to participate in the planning as a
key to achieving the outcome rather than simply having a plan to work by. Participation
is also found in the exercise of planning. Meaning is negotiated between what is in the
plan and its enactment (participation). Participating in the planned project is not all that
happens in a project – e.g. preparing for status review meetings, and keeping key
stakeholders informally on-board. Meaning of the project is potentially negotiated in
discussions of project objectives/scope. The planning reified in the plan document is
participated within the actions taken in the project. Plans are left-brain friendly while
planning and enactment/participation are right-brain notions.

An Overall Capability for Mastering Project Management

In order to master project management one needs to start with a basic set of
knowledge about what is required to manage projects. One also needs to be able to use
the knowledge (practice with it), in ways that are separated from actual performance.
Also needed are ways to increase knowledge beyond the basics so meaning can be found
to build expertise, and increase mastery learning. Meaning can be negotiated within a

CoP. And finally, the mastery capability needs to be deployed through a CoP within enterprises so they can see vast improvements in achieving success with projects.

Four steps toward achieving project management mastery are:

1. Acquire a set of knowledge that embodies the notion of project management that can be built upon.
2. Be able to use the knowledge to practice project management separate from actually managing a real project.
3. Participate in an on-going group that is dedicated toward project management mastery such as a CoP.
4. Get individual enterprises on-board with the idea. A CoP can be employed on multiple levels and the organizational/enterprise level is very important. A facilitating extra-enterprise CoP dedicated to mastery, through the university, can be a good launch vehicle and support mechanism, but enterprise adoption is where it may have its greatest impact.

Project management is a discipline that requires knowledge, understanding, and a devotion to a path of mastery. Without knowledge we are attempting solutions in the dark, without understanding we know what to do but can't do it successfully most of the time. Many, such as Benjamin Bloom have indicated the path up learning requires steps along the way. These steps can be seen as advancing from apprentice to journeyman to master. Learning is facilitated if one recognizes the need for a mastery approach. There will be no methodology that can serve as a magic bullet making the novice a master. The path of mastery requires one to practice along the way. The parametric analysis is a way to both practice project management recognition skills, as well as build expertise from one actual experience to another. The project management master will be able to diagnose a project and act on his/her learned expertly formed intuition to reach project completions that are successful.

PART TWO

Primary/Filtering Parameters

Since there are so many possibilities for managing a project, one needs to have a way to determine what actually needs serious consideration. Some parameters set the stage for which other parameters should be considered "in play" or important enough to be given specific attention by the project manager. These primary parameters filter out unimportant parameters, thus reducing the overall complexity and effort needed to understand a project. There are four primary/filtering parameters. These are: *Basics* (see chapter two), *intentions* (chapter two), *organizational context* (chapter three), and *project aspects* (chapter four).

The other thing these parameters provide is a way to refine the practice of broad interpretation. A project manager, when starting with primary/filtering parameters, actually gains an initial understanding of the project. This initial understanding may be the most important part about learning how to manage it.

The parametric approach provides a way to practice or learn about what it takes to manage a project along with a way to integrate that knowledge. It also provides a way to communicate about a project to others - what went right/wrong, and most importantly, WHY.

The *basics* parameter of a project (see chapter two) represents the first primary/filtering parameter. This parameter focuses attention on the weakness of any project by explicitly stating what makes a particular effort a project. It's the first attempt to describe the project. These eight *basics* will provide a boundary for further interpretation of the project. Changing one of these *basics* often means changing the project significantly. *Basics* and project scope go hand in hand.

Chapter one depicted the sixteen parameters used to describe project management. The four primary parameters inform the project manager which of the remaining twelve are worth considering, or are "in play" for managing the project to success. The remaining chapters highlight these parameters, culminating in Part Six which integrates them together in a complete analysis.

Chapter 2

Basics and Intentions Analysis

Basic Ingredients of a Project (*Basics*)

Basketball allows you to take steps with the ball as long as you pound it on the ground while moving – the skill of dribbling is basic to basketball. You can play basketball without dribbling but a great deal of potential play is lost. Project managers should know the basics of what makes a project or their managerial performance could suffer. Project *basics* can be revealed by a simple exercise. Think of a prime example of a project, or what we could call a paradigm case. I've conducted this exercise many times in the classroom and three examples are inevitably mentioned: Building a house, erecting the pyramids in Egypt, and conducting a space launch. By examining what each of these has in common we reveal the common parameters of a project – the project *basics*. These *basics* are better than a definition because definitions are limited by their circularity. We understand concepts better by analogy than definitions (Ossorio, 1981). *Basics* are at the root of what we identify as a project, and missing one or more is asking for trouble. Missing one or more of these really means you don't have a full-blown project, and attempting to manage it as such will be a struggle – like playing basketball without dribbling. Knowing which *basics* are missing will inform you of possible problems the project will face.

The following statement highlights the eight *basics* of a project. A project has a *beginning* and an *end* along with an *objective*. It uses multiple and *quantifiable* finite *resources* like time, money, and people. It requires a *leader*, co-exists with *other projects* that vie for the same resources, and is actually a *research* effort (see Figures 2.1 and 2.2).

Basic	Description
Beginning	Formal or informal kickoff. The first unit of work initiated.
End	The final deliverable is accomplished, no more changes to the project.
Objective	The overall goal of the project. The significance of the final deliverable.
Resources - Time	The amount of time the project takes from beginning to end. Time that could be spent on other things.
- Money	The amount of money the project costs to produce, or work toward the final deliverable.
- People	People involved in the project work – either directly or indirectly (stakeholders).
Quantifiable	The resources and time of a project can be measured.
Leader	Person responsible for completion of the work on the project.
Other Projects	Other projects that use similar or the same resources.
Research	The project represents something new or innovative. The effort has a research air.

A Project's Primary Parameters – The Basics
Figure 2.1

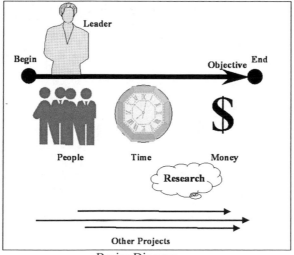

Basics Diagram
Figure 2.2

Projects of Life – Getting to Work (using the *basics*)

This project begins when I arise from slumber and ends when I sit down at my desk ready for a meeting with two other faculty members. My *objective* in this project of life is to get to work on time for the meeting. Between the *beginning* and *end* are all the activities of this project. These include getting myself physically prepared (showering, dressing, etc.), preparing and consuming a hearty breakfast of bacon, eggs, toast, juice, and coffee – or perhaps just a cup of yogurt, a granola bar, and decaf coffee. Collecting and checking the contents of my bag, making my way to the car, and then driving to the university. Once there, finding a place to park and walking to the office.

I need *resources* to accomplish this project such as clothing, food, car, streets, knowledge, skill, time, and money (for gas). I need to be able to measure (*quantify*) the project in order to leave on time, plus the project will require innovative thinking in case the usual path to work is clogged with cars from people running their own "getting to work" projects (*other efforts* vying for the same street resources). I cannot rely on anyone else to pull this project off but myself. I am the formal *leader* and can blame only myself (or traffic) if I'm late for the meeting.

Next day, Saturday, it looks like the same project takes place but it's not. On this particular Saturday the *objective* is to get to class on time, but if I'm late the students are much more forgiving than the faculty I met with the day before. I'll need to be *innovative* because the street usage *resource* will be different. Most sane people find Saturday much better for sleeping-in rather than going to work. The project will differ in other ways. I'll dress differently, may not clean up as much, and grab coffee along with a sausage and egg sandwich from a convenient drive through restaurant.

In the course of everyday life we execute projects without giving them a second thought. We've mastered these projects, and can master any project as well as the whole idea of project management itself. Everyone has this mastery capability if they're provided frameworks to understand the phenomena along with the chance to practice with these frameworks.

Intentions Parameter

After an initial project proposal but before the project begins an intentions analysis will provide the project manager additional insight concerning the project. This intentions analysis is suggested in order to make sure stakeholders know the initial and subsequent reasons for a project initiative. The analysis will provide an answer to the questions of what is wanted from the project and why (or its significance), and how to go about managing it based on these results.

Worldviews and Intentions

The results of an intentions analysis will help focus the project manager's attention on different project goals and enable the setting of realistic expectations. Consider the three worldviews mentioned in chapter one -- the world of *machines*, the *strategic* world, and the world of *people*. Each worldview has its own primary elements, key processes, and an explicit or implied overall goal (Putman, 1988). The primary elements for a *machine* worldview are technologies, operational tactics, and product-oriented representations. For the *strategic* world elements include financial results, overall quantitative representations of the business, and other measures used for comparative or planning purposes. For the world of *people* primary elements are people, groups, and cultures. The critical process for the *machine* world is performance, for the *strategy* world calculation, and for the people world it's behavior.

But how does identifying a project worldview help the project manager discover the real intention or value of his/her project? I made a presentation to a university's education department explaining project intentions and used an example of teaching geography in schools with video technology. I asked the key question: Why do you want to teach geography using video technology? Responding to my own question with: "I don't know," I got chuckles and nodding of heads from the educators because they claimed a lot of "new programs" in many school districts are started with no one knowing their value – this is an example of an *experimental* intention.. Another answer offered could be because teachers are wasting a lot of time copying maps, and various charts before school negatively impacting their teaching time and energy. They could be much more efficient if they could use this new technology. It would improve their *process* of teaching (the *process* intention). This made sense to the educators as well. Another answer offered was many schools are in steep competition for the best students, and if a school in another part of town were to use this technology, ours would be looked upon as "old hat" and less effective and therefore lose part of their market. This is a *strategic intention* for using video technology in the classroom. Once again the teachers understood this and were able to relate it to other innovations of which they had been a part. The fourth possible answer could be to change the assumptions and beliefs teachers have about their professional role. Teachers come to work in the morning and barely find their way to the teachers lounge and see their fellow teachers demoralized, sick, and worn out from the same old grind. This technology may reinvigorate them and initiate a self reexamination of their professional role. This is a *cultural intention*. The educators were a bit reluctant to see this, but could identify with other changes that had worked to make teaching better for some professionals in ways not necessarily related to productivity.

The unique feature of each world view focuses the project manager's attention on different project goals (see Figure 2.3).

World View	Primary Elements	Key Process	Related Characteristics	Overall Goal
Machines	- Technologies - Operational tactics - Product re-presentations	Performance	Quality Efficiencies Inventions Diffusion	Efficiency
Strategy	- Financial results - Quantitative reps - Measures for planning	Impact	Bottom line Variation Audit	Outcome or Impact
People	- People - Groups - Cultures	Behavior	Relationships Identity Motives	Meaning

World Views
Figure 2.3

Identifying Intentions

Three questions are helpful for identifying intentions.

      1. What is wanted from this project?

      2. What is the significance of the project (why is it wanted)?

      3. How should decisions/choices be made about the project?

Results of answering these questions will reveal an intention for *experimental* action, *process* improvement, *strategic* impact, or *cultural* change. An *experimental* action means the project contains a great deal of unknowns and may not meet a specified objective. Its significance is for innovation, invention, or finding new viewpoints. A *process* improvement is about improving a process by making it more efficient, or more effective. The significance of a *process* improvement is quality, timeliness, or to make things possible that were not before. A *strategic* impact is concerned with how the goal will affect the overall enterprise. Its significance may be market share, and/or survival in the external environment (market). A *cultural* change is remaking the way people normally go about their activities, what they may consider acceptable behaviors. The acceptability may be related to human feelings or attitudes about what is important. The significance of a *cultural* change is to remake the assumptions and values by which people co-exist in an environment.

Decisions and choices differ across the intentions. Projects with *experimental intentions* use a choice process that is systemic. It relates to the system of innovation and how it unfolds. Choices are made "on the fly" in this system of entrepreneurial thought and fluid expectations. The systemic choice principle is also used within a *cultural intention*. Culture relates to the system of people and their acceptable behaviors. These choices involve individuals and how they act in groups. A human group system sets the groundwork for how choices are made. Sometimes decisions are made simply because everyone espouses its obvious benefits and are afraid to reveal weaknesses (an example is *Groupthink* (Janis, 1982)). *Calculated* choice principles are used in *process* and *strategic intentions* because process changes and strategic expectations are usually quantifiable, leading to project decisions focused on the quantifiable outcomes. If one can establish quantifiable outcome expectations, the planning and activities to achieve the outcome are often set up in somewhat strict quantifiable ways. Decisions are often made based on how much, how many, and when to expect a deliverable. We've often heard" If you can't measure it, you can't manage it." This comment is grounded in *strategic* or *process intentions* (see Figure 2.4)

An *experimental* action would involve a project that is fundamentally research and would have an overall objective of discovery. Once the discovery is found the project is finished. It may lead to other projects or it may not. The way to manage this kind of project is through

Intention	Want	Significance	Choice Principle
Experimental	Unclear	Discovery	Systemic
Process	Efficiency, Effectiveness	Cost, Quality	Calculated
Strategic	Business Impact	Business Advantage	Calculated
Cultural	Organizational change	Assumptions values altered	Systemic

Basis of Intentions
Figure 2.4

informal feedback with few measures taken during the project. For *process* improvement projects the ultimate goal is reached through detail planning and monitoring, and usually measured through a *calculated* method such as cost-benefit analysis (e.g. remodel the assembly line to produce products more efficiently). *Strategic* impact projects have objectives at the enterprise-level, and are managed using milestones and managerial feedback mechanisms. They are usually associated with some risk and are often carried out with a handpicked team. Their goal is measured against market impact (e.g. implementation of a critical new product). *Culture* change projects usually involve a large group, and a lengthy process that changes as ideas move in and out of importance. It's also hard to measure their impact or plan them at a detail level.

Intentions and Choices

Making choices on projects can involve direct calculation by measuring outcomes based on acceptable metrics. Another way choices can be made is systemically. Criteria for these choices unfold as the project moves forward. For *experimental* and *culture* change projects the choice principle is *systemic*, and for *process* and *strategic* projects the choice principle is *calculated*. For projects whose *intention* is *process* improvement the acceptable measurement is usually set out ahead of time and becomes a part of the project plan incorporating measures of time, money and resources as represented in Gantt charts, resource histograms, and cumulative cost curves. For *strategic*-intentioned projects the choice principle is also *calculated*, but at the milestone or overall project level, and is associated with value and business impact rather than cost-payback. Strategic changes can be accounted for by using the five forces of a market (Porter, 1985). These are shown in

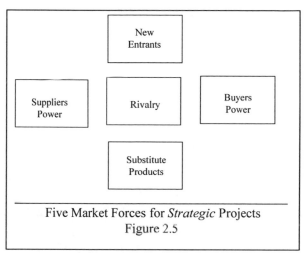

New
Entrants

Suppliers
Power

Rivalry

Buyers
Power

Substitute
Products

Five Market Forces for *Strategic* Projects
Figure 2.5

Figure 2.5. One way to account for strategic impact is to assess the change against each of the forces.

For *experimental* projects the way one chooses to go forward is dependent on the step just taken, and therefore the principles are part of a broader system of ideas associated with the project. For *culture* change projects a broader system should also be considered. The culture is evolving and it contains the principles by which choices are made. Therefore the method of choosing unfolds as the project unfolds (see Figure 2.6). A questionnaire for analyzing intentions is provided in appendix C.

Intention	Project Planning	Requirements Discovery	Review Level
Experimental	Set up environment	Unfolding	Cyclical or only at end
Process	Detail tasks	Analysis and design	Schedule at tasks
Strategic	Milestones	Opportunity search	Milestone
Cultural	Milestones	Assumptions surfacing	Periodic assessments

Intentions and Project Dynamics
Figure 2.6

Inconsistent Intentions

Intentions of a project can change over time. As projects become more or less exposed to various stakeholders these projects may change in their overall expected outcomes. Also, different stakeholders may have differing perspectives on the real intention of the project. It's not unlikely that many projects start off as *experimental*, and then move into a consideration for *process* improvement, eventually requiring a *cultural* change in order to make the *strategic* impact that may mean survival for the enterprise. At each intention change step, the project should change in managerial approach and expectations.

		Assumed Intentions			
		Experimental	**Process**	**Strategic**	**Cultural**
Actual Intentions	**Experimental**	Aligned	7	8	10
	Process	1	Aligned	9	11
	Strategic	2	4	Aligned	12
	Cultural	3	5	6	Aligned

Actual vs. Assumed Intentions
Figure 2.7

The diagonal in Figure 2.7 shows assumed and actual intentions aligned. This is not always the case. Misalignment can happen for a variety of reasons. Those below the diagonal of alignment are numbered from 1-6. These "off-diagonal" intentions usually present more difficult problems for the project manager than those above the diagonal (numbered 7-12), because expectations of project outcomes are of greater impact than assumed to be the case. More is expected of the project manager for *process* improvement than for projects that are *experimental* (this does not mean the deliverable of an *experimental* project is insignificant, it's about the project's managerial expectation of stakeholders). More is expected of *strategic* projects than *process* projects since their impact is in some way critical to the enterprise, and still more is expected of *cultural* change projects because they connect with the fundamental assumptions and values people use to accomplish their work. More is expected of the project manager as *intentions* get tougher because the outcome impact of these projects increases. When a project gains approval through a diligent process it's assumed the way the project was described is actually the case. Many projects have to go through budgetary processes resulting in over-optimistic promised payback often to just secure the funding. The project may actually be *experimental* but had to be approved as a *process* because there is no other way to get it approved. The thought that the Panama Canal was simply a *process* project about digging a trench between oceans would be replaced with an *experimental* approach due to the uniqueness of the effort. Many times the way a project is subsequently managed is according to what was initially offered as a description, but not what it actually is. The actual versus assumed nature of a project may be the same or different.

Below the alignment diagonal (cells 1-6)

When a project is assumed to be less, in impact, than is actually the case (below the diagonal), it will tend to be under managed and cause major problems. These projects below the alignment diagonal are described in the following paragraphs (with the aid of a few analogies), and potential remedies are proposed for each.

1. Deer in the Headlights (Assumed *experimental intention* but actually *process intention*)

On a summer evening, driving one of my family members home 120 miles away, we come over a hill and there stands a deer caught in the headlights. I've heard too many "deer in the headlights" stories to expect him to move, and I also remembered most severe deer accidents happen because the driver runs off the road. So I give the deer all the room I can without leaving the highway. When examining the car in the next town under good light I see there are several hairs left by the lucky deer (not to mention the lucky passengers). The deer, though he could stroll willy-nilly, ended up on a path (the highway) dedicated to a particular process (auto traffic).

For situations where the project is actually about *process* improvement but are being managed as if they are *experimental* will usually be disastrous like deer wandering into a well organized transportation system. Changes will be made without appropriate review and whimsical opinions of stakeholders may change the project objective without adequate review. The solution to this off-diagonal is for the project manager to institute a planning and review process and a formal change management process making sure all the stakeholders know the importance of these items. Also, the project manager should plan for expansion and gate-keep the new process initiative using a controlled roll-out.

Web site development may fall victim to the *deer in the headlights* situation. The web site may be needed to accept new orders from customers, but technologists may be changing the look and feel of the site as well as the technical infrastructure without appropriate approvals. Some people may even refuse to use the web site because its navigation is counter-intuitive. This coupled with an abundance of misspelled words may leave the whole process questionable in the customers' eyes.

2. Management by Walking Around (Assumed *experimental intention* but actually *strategic*)

When the business is in danger a manager with a walking around mentality may be looking for internal creative ways to solve a problem that exists in the market or external environment. Projects that are assumed to have an *experimental intention* but are actually *strategic* are critically dangerous for the business. They expose the business to unwarranted risks and may impact the business in such unexpected ways that the project may eventually be stopped and reexamined and may result in a new project team being assigned.

A new project team is considered because the old team may be judged as not focusing on the real objective of the project and attempting too many innovative solutions. A key stakeholder committee made up of senior management and affected business units is suggested. By involving key stakeholders, the project objective can be made clear, along with how the project results will specially impact the business. The committee should meet immediately to clear up the real intention for the project.

3. Frankenstein's Monster (Assumed *experimental intention* but actually *cultural*)

Just as Frankenstein thought his "new man" was a grand experiment, others didn't see it that way. The wonders and anxieties of the unknown result in many projects failing for lack of sensitivity to their people-oriented dynamic environment. For projects assumed to be *experimental* that are actually *cultural,* the outside stakeholders will tend to be ignored. Co-locating the project team with these stakeholders will provide one solution to this off-diagonal. Also getting some of the key stakeholders assigned to the project team full-time could be helpful to dispel the mystery and anxiety. When people are critical for acceptance of the project deliverable they should be involved early and often to get and maintain "buy-in".

4. Britannica Bust (Assumed *process intention* but actually *strategic*)

There's no doubt that Britannica was the best encyclopedia for a long time. Yet this high quality, top of the line product was basically done in by Microsoft with its Encarta digital encyclopedia. Families spending roughly $1,000 to educate junior chose to spend it on a computer with a "good enough" encyclopedia rather than a nice set of Britannica's bound volumes (Evans, 1997).

If the project is assumed to be *process* when it is actually *strategic* the outside stakeholders need to review the project ASAP. The result may take a significant part of your business away. The value of the project to the enterprise should be specifically identified and communicated to all other stakeholders as well.

5. Jurassic Park Syndrome (Assumed *process intention* but actually *cultural*)

For projects that are actually *cultural* but are assumed to be *process* we have the Jurassic Park Syndrome – the world of the project is thought to be like building Disney World where crowds and machinery are controlled through creative design, but what's really taking place is very dynamic with the project continually being redefined by its own outcomes as it unfolds. There are clear espoused objectives that sound very reasonable but are too narrow. The project's objective has been made much too rational.

A project with a cultural intention will produce results that are usually unpredictable at the outset. They will evolve as interactions with people and circumstances occur. The solution is to broaden the objective and to involve as many outside ideas as possible and continually seek stakeholder understanding.

6. Bay of Pigs (Assumed *strategic intention* but actually *cultural*)

The decision to launch an attack on Cuba using exiled Cubans was disastrous. President Kennedy met with his advisors and they all agreed it was a go. Yet many of them personally felt the situation was too dynamic to take such a risk. But since the effort was strategic to the country, and Kennedy provided strong leadership, they didn't air their opinions (Janis, 1982). When the actual project is *cultural* and it's assumed to be *strategic* the evolutionary nature of the project will be lost by emphasizing the organizational-market impact. Subtleties will be overlooked and a "just get on with it" attitude will prevail. Flexibility for the culture to remake itself will be lost resulting in a key deliverable that will fail.

The project manager should continually bring the dynamics into focus and question what the project objective is and how it is being met. Changes will occur, and how all stakeholders interpret these needs to be determined. A series of milestones should be established to bring people together, not to reconfirm what is supposed to happen, but to determine what is happening now and to change the objective of the project to meet this new reality. Some would argue that this *cultural* project assumed to be *strategic* is the most potentially disastrous. It's easy to confirm the activities meet the objective but everyone "groupthinks" their way through while not challenging initial assumptions as in the Bay of Pigs disaster. When groupthink occurs, a mind-guard needs to be set up to challenge prevailing opinion avoiding early consensus.

Above the alignment diagonal (cells 7-12)

When a project is assumed to be more, in terms of its impact, than is actually the case (above the diagonal), it will tend to be over managed, and perhaps too much consideration given to the wrong stakeholders.

7. Micro-managing (Assumed *process intention* but actually *experimental*)

In an *experimental* project that is trying to abide by the strict project management disciplines of "on time, within budget, and using planned resources", the expected innovative result will be stifled due to micro-management efforts. The solution to this off-diagonal is to reduce the controlling factors being used to track progress, and reduce the number of people involved that have little or nothing to do with the actually content of the project's objective.

One job for the project manager is to monitor, even gate-keep, the communication between everyone involved. If you have a project management set of guidelines that focus on *process* improvement projects (which is often the case), an *experimental* project needs to be an exception to these guidelines.

8. Over-politicking (Assumed *strategic intention* but actually *experimental*)

For this off-diagonal project the team will usually be viewed as unproductive. They are being measured on impact but the project is too innovative to demonstrate impact. The project leader may be devoting too much time and attention to politicking with outside stakeholders and not enough to the performance of the team. The project team should be removed from outside stakeholders' considerations and be freed to work toward an innovative solution. The project objective may be too specific and will need to be made less confining.

9. Management by Airplane Magazine (Assumed *strategic intention* but actually *process*)

During a three-hour plane trip the CEO grabs the airline magazine in the seat pocket in front of him and begins to read about how a company succeeded with a new way of doing business using the web. Upon his return to the office, he calls in his team together and tells them they should launch such an initiative. It's a localized process improvement problem that requires several realignments of current processes. Since the CEO is removed from this kind of knowledge the problem seems more daunting than it really is.

Projects that are assumed to be *strategic* but are actually *process* will result in more attention being paid to business impact rather than reaching the localized improvement needed. Too much time will be spent with outside stakeholders in efforts to connect to a business strategy when no strategy may be directly supported. Unrealistic objectives will be identified and may be used to sell the project. Post project reviews will be frustrating because what was promised will not clearly be delivered. The objective usually misses the mark because a connection to the business is too ethereal and those that could make the connection are either not involved or give the objective a polite nod without due consideration. Once a business impact is mentioned as a possible objective, the project will be anchored there even if the real objective is to meet a localized process improvement. This is succumbing to the anchoring and adjustment bias where people tend to get anchored to a point and adjust in small moves from it even if the actual situation is far removed from this point (Tversky, 1974).

These projects need to be reassessed to make sure the objective is realistic. A meeting with the project team should be a first step, followed by a meeting with key stakeholders. The meeting's major agenda item should be how to identify specifically if the objective can be met, and what meeting the objective means to the key stakeholders. If a business impact objective is eventually possible, then it should be addressed in a future project, or this project will need to be re-planned to meet the business objective. More time will usually be required to make sure the outside stakeholders are adequately involved throughout the project. Victims of this off-diagonal often see the results as scope-creep.

10. Over-clinging (Assumed *cultural intention* but actually *experimental*)

These projects will be characterized by over devotion/attention to the project team and their interactions with one another as well as with the rest of the stakeholders. It's like clinging too tightly to the young person that needs some freedom. The project needs to be moved off site if possible, or at least located separately from outside influences. The project manager could hold a brainstorming meeting with the team on what possible objectives the project should have, list the strengths and weaknesses of each objective, then gain consensus on the top two or three. The team members should produce action plans for the next step for reaching each objective. Fear and anxiety may be indicative of team members in these projects.

11. The Cowardly Lion (Assumed *cultural intention* but actually *process*)

On these projects more attention is paid to the possible implications of reaching the objective than to managing the project to reach it. It could be fear, like the cowardly lion in the *Wizard of Oz*, or just being oversensitive when the situation calls for action rather than sensitivity. The project objective should be made real clear then a solid plan formulated to reach it. To solve this off-diagonal problem the number of meetings with outside constituents should be kept at a minimum, change control disciplines should be established as much as the project deliverable requirements allow, and information sharing outside the immediate project team discouraged.

12. Hansel and Gretel Miscue (Assumed *cultural intention* but actually *strategic*)

On these projects the proper measures have not been established, nor has the objective been made as clear as it needs to be. Hansel and Gretel judged being at ease with the "little lady with cookies" along with their minor consideration for a return (bread crumbs) was sufficient. Their feel for what was happening was insufficient, but more importantly they had no strategy for what was actually happening. One remedy is to provide opportunities for key external stakeholders to address the project team and other stakeholders concerning the impact and importance of the project for the enterprise, and then reconfirm the project's objective and how it will be measured. Impact on the enterprise should be constantly stressed.

The prudent project manager should continually keep asking the intentions question to maintain a realistic and optimal goal. The analogies may keep the off-diagonals in mind (see Figure 2.8). An intention check should be made at project review meetings, and communicated to relevant stakeholders.

		Assumed Intentions			
		Experimental	Process	Strategic	Cultural
Actual Intentions	Experimental	Aligned	7 Micro managing	8 Over- politicking	10 Over- clinging
	Process	1 Deer in Headlights	Aligned	9 Management by airplane mag.	11 The cowardly lion
	Strategic	2 Management by Walking	4 Britannica Bust	Aligned	12 Hansel and Gretel
	Cultural	3 Frankenstein's Monster	5 Jurassic Park	6 Bay of Pigs	Aligned

Actual vs. Assumed Intentions with Names
Figure 2.8

A starting place for understanding a project is to identify its overall *intention*. Knowing a project's intention will reveal to the project manager a basis by which project team members are going to work, as well as the expectations of major stakeholders. *Intention* analysis can serve as an early warning signal about misalignment of thoughts about the project and its overall impact. It can expose disagreements about the expected impact as well as identify where assumptions about the project's overall impact may have been made incorrectly by certain individuals or groups.

The effective project manager needs to get a project launched as early as possible, but it needs to be headed in the right overall direction. *Intentions* are a way to uncover what people really expect of the project's outcome thus narrowing the requirements domain and making the project plan more realistic. A project charter should include a good intentions analysis. Confusion over the project's impact may occur during project execution in which case another *intentions* analysis ought to be performed (see Figure 2.9).

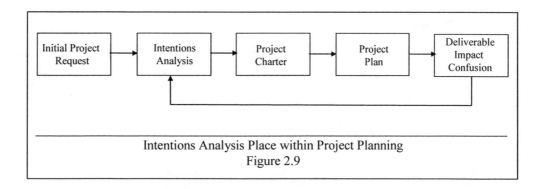

Intentions Analysis Place within Project Planning
Figure 2.9

Chapter 3

Organizational Context

Just as every bird has its nest and every bee has its comb, every project has a context within which certain rules and behaviors are expected or taken-for-granted. An enterprise context can reveal more about the project's viability than all the Gantt charts in the world. It provides a way the project can be understood so that more effective decisions can be made, proper channels of communication can be established with stakeholders, and appropriate leadership can be applied. Many times the context of a project goes unexamined because it's assumed everyone knows it. This may work out fine if the project participants all implicitly understand its context, and the results of the project are not expected to change the context. The prudent project manager may not want to rely on luck, but overtly examine the project's context.

Systems Thinking

From a system thinking point of view organizational context is a suprasystem to the project. Context includes the important assumptions members of the enterprise have as to how a project could be interpreted. As some may recall from an introductory physics course the game of pool is a good example of the laws of force and momentum. If you strike the balls the same way the reactions should be exactly the same – all other things being equal. The problem is all other things are *never* equal, and hence the laws are more rules-of-thumb that seem to work for most elementary engineering problems. If we are on board a ship tossing to and fro on the high seas, the game of pool may have to be played differently or under new rules. (Perhaps you can only play in calm seas). The context is often more important than the particulars of the game. This is true for a project as well.

The context will color opinions for how a project is accepted or not by the various stakeholders. Without this interpretation the project manager may be caught by surprise by many decisions and attitudes. If every context is assumed the same across all projects, then what works in one should work in another. This is not the case. Projects not only vary because of their very nature as research undertakings, but because of the context within which they are carried out. If you could construct the same project in two different contexts they would have to be managed differently.

Four ways for describing an enterprise context are provided. Even though there is overlap between these, each has its own focus. The four are:

1. Decision Atmosphere
2. Dominant Organizing Competitive Imperative
3. Management/Operations Interaction Assumptions
4. Organizational Image

Decision Atmosphere

Leadership of a project requires decision-making, and understanding the atmosphere in which these decisions are made. Assumptions about decision-making produce enterprises that function differently. Three decision atmospheres are worth considering. The first is where management provides overall control and authority for almost everything that happens. This is an *autocratic* form of leadership where the communication is mostly from the leader to the subordinate. *Autocratic* suggests a highly structured form of organizing the work where the seat of authority is at the top. This is a very efficient way to make decisions, but may not be very effective if shared information within and across management structures is needed.

Centralized power structures often dominate in enterprises where their founder is an active leader. To many people in the organization the decisions may seem more emotional than rational, but due to the centralized power that has proven successful over time, the decisions are trusted and many times sought out by other key leaders. Project decisions may take longer unless the power structure is adequately addressed. For the project manager it's as important to communicate with the centralized power structure as with the key recipients of the project's deliverables. The downside of a well connected project is acting too quickly. Decisions, though perhaps ill-informed, are acted on before adequate thought is given. When the founder leaves, retires, changes positions within the enterprise, decisions become very conservative and much second guessing occurs. The project manager will need to provide a lot of justification for decisions made in this environment (Siehl, 1985).

The second atmosphere is *democratic*. In this form everyone is considered equal. Leaders provide opportunities for collaborative decision-making. The workday may consist of a lot of meetings where consensus is sought. The exchange of ideas between leaders and subordinates is on an equal authority plane. Asking the operational people how to improve and providing over all leadership and support to these improvements is common. Information is exchanged with a broad range of participants and gathering points of view before decisions are made is a common practice. One key behavior for the project manager is to ensure people merely interested, as well as key stakeholders are kept informed. This takes constant checking through meetings, phone calls, hallway encounters, etc. Face-to-face is the best mechanism. Formal approaches may not work because people may have learned to ignore these kind of communications until something goes wrong (sending a formal status review memo may not be adequate).

In the third atmosphere decisions are expected to be a part of the job itself, and leaders, for the most part, are "hands off". There's a residual hierarchical leadership only for overall coordination. This form of decision making has been known as empowerment and taking place in clustering work groups, self-managed work teams, etc. Be careful the residual hierarchy does not intrude on project decisions. They should be kept informed but not to actively participate in project decisions. Authority, in this last *lassez faire* atmosphere, when perceived to come from the top, often meets with real resistance and can stop any initiative before its gets off the ground. Decision-making is up to the people performing the work. This is most effective in enterprises that have heavy research components where information is shared only as broadly as the task demands. The project manager's major concern in this context is to keep decisions from becoming too whimsical. Quick status meetings, or "stand up" meetings at the beginning of the day, can keep people on the same page and reduce decision conflicts.

Dominant Organizing Competitive Imperative

Every enterprise has a dominant way it competes. If we put this into a historical perspective we can see how this dominant way may provide insight into what is happening in an enterprise and why it is happening in a certain fashion. In the western part of the world companies lived through a time where demand was much greater than supply. After World War II industry was set up for the war and not for consumer products. When the war ended and GIs returned home, they were looking to purchase toasters and not tanks. There weren't enough toasters. Hence every toaster that could be made could be sold. With this as the reality, companies concentrated on production efficiency, not on customer relationships or product quality. After all, everything built would sell, so why worry about customers? Customers were considered almost a nuisance.

As enterprises across the world changed (e.g. the rebuilding of Japan and Germany), international competition became more prevalent, and soon, supply outstripped demand. The imperative changed from production to service and quality. Strategies on how to compete became hot topics (e.g. competing on low cost or product niche), and businesses began to reorganize into teams, and implemented such things as quality circles. Along with this new mindset came updated and new technologies that enabled differing ways to build, manage, and improve the products themselves. With a quantum leap in computing and communication resources, new ways to do business became possible (e.g. competing with information).

Through this historical perspective three distinct imperatives come out. The first is the *classical* production imperative where demand is greater than supply; the second, a *modern* imperative where supply is greater than demand; and the third, when the imperative is *changing* from *classic* to *modern* (often called Business Process Reengineering – BPR) (Hammer, 1990). Another variant to changing is from *modern* to *classic*. This last imperative is important for many projects since the project itself may be the vehicle by which the context is being changed (see Figure 3.1).

Projects in the *classical* (quadrant 1 in Figure 2.1) organization concentrate on planning, control, and execution of the project. They usually

		This Project	
Context		Classic	Modern
	Classic	1-Stable	4- Changing
	Modern	3- Changing	2-Org Effectiveness

Organizing Imperative
Figure 3.1

have objectives that increase the enterprise's efficiency or production capacity. The environment is stable and managing projects is predominantly sticking to a plan laid out ahead of time. Projects in *modern* (quadrant 2) organizations are monitored by milestones and usually have lax controls. Their objectives often deal with making the enterprise more effective in their market, or differentiating their product/services. Critical for managing projects in this environment is to listen to and inform key stakeholders. Projects that are in a *changing* (quadrant 3) environment meet with heavy resistance by process owners, have goals that are clear but hard to maintain, and are surrounded by people that will say, "We never did it that way before". The primary issues here for project managers is to stick to the objective, and build a constituency that will support the project in the face of heavy resistance. Enterprises in the midst of changing are often unstable and traditional approaches may not work, the project stakeholders may even be hard to identify. In extreme instances, one may find projects with no clear leader, or where the leadership role has changed numerous times. Projects in *changing* (quadrant 4) environments going from modern to classic could be part of an organizational merger. Many stakeholders may see this as a step backward. The project manager needs to reveal the overall need for effective communication between what were two different organizations. It's a survival issue not an organizing one (see Figure 3.2).

If you are managing a project in the *classic* (quadrant 1) (and hence are called production imperative) environment, plan the project in as much detail as possible, report at the detail task level, make sure the

Organizational Context Model Parameter	Parametric Values
Decision Atmosphere	Autocratic Democratic Lassez faire
Dominant Organizing Imperative	Classical Modern Changing (BPR)
Management/Operations Interactions	Mechanistic Organic

Organizational Context Parameters
Figure 3.2

budget is established up front, and acquire the resources before establishing the project plan. This should be a two-step process: One, use the resources (people) to build a plan and then get it approved; two, execute the project according to its detailed plan. Monitor the project at the task level and make sure critical tasks are getting priority. You may want to employ project management software to aid in the planning and monitoring of the project.

If the project is in a *modern* (quadrant 2) environment some interaction will probably be necessary between the initial plan step and the execution step. What's most important is to deliver the greatest value to the enterprise and not be constrained entirely by a previous plan or budget. Projects in this environment tend to take longer and cost more than initial plans identified because their success is measured at the bottom line impact not against a predetermined plan. Managing by milestones may be more prudent since many tasks could change during the project's execution.

In the *changing* (quadrants 3 and 4) environment significant resistance will be encountered and a planning/execution two-step process will be frustrated at the detail level. However, planning should be done as a separate step to set up the environment for change. This does not involve detail task planning, but enacting changes by appealing to those is critical social change roles. These include opinion leader, change agent, innovator, change aid, and change target (Rogers, 1983). Another step-one planning action is to surface the change *assumptions* of major stakeholders. These assumptions are

magic bullet (the technology result itself will produce the change), *advocate* to push for the change to push it it (sell it within the organization), and *facilitator* where the organization is setup for the change first and pulled into place (Markus, 1993) (see Figure 3.3).

Assumption	Action
Magic Bullet	Let it happen
Advocate	Push it in
Facilitator	Pull it in

Change Assumptions
Figure 3.3

Management /Operations Interaction Assumptions

A study conducted several decades ago reported on how some companies behave in what was termed, *mechanistic* ways, while others behaved in *organic* ways. The *mechanistic* verses *organic* distinction is about how the organizations were assumed to work, both in their management control structure and their operations production capability (Burns and Stalker, 1961). *Mechanistic* is a term used to imply the enterprise works as a cog/wheel type machine. People in *mechanistic* enterprises know their specific tasks and functions and perform them with machine efficiency. One does not need to know why the machine works, or what it produces, only how to do one's job. Tasks are well defined, management structure is rigid and hierarchical, little flexibility is provided, authoritarian decision-making style is employed, and communication occurs from the top to the bottom of the hierarchy. Most *mechanistic* enterprises have a command/control form of leadership, and little feedback is either sought or given. With the organization in stable environments and a work force that is constant, a *mechanistic* enterprise may be the most effective.

The *organic* enterprise functions like an organism made up of a lose collection of subsystems. One subsystem may change its functioning relatively independent of the others. *Organic* enterprises are characterized by flexibility, control is within each subsystem, tasks that are very broadly defined, and everyone knowing the overall goal of the enterprise. The *organic* enterprise is one that self-adapts to changes, where the changes may be initiated anywhere inside or outside the enterprise.

Projects within a *mechanistic* enterprise are usually tightly controlled, are expected to come in on time and within budget, usually have an objective that deals with efficiency or increased control over existing resources. Projects within an *organic* enterprise are usually managed with relatively little planning and loose controls, although large projects or those requiring many integration points may require tight controls. Their objectives may be described in broad terms, as in R&D, and have more to do with value to particular parts of the

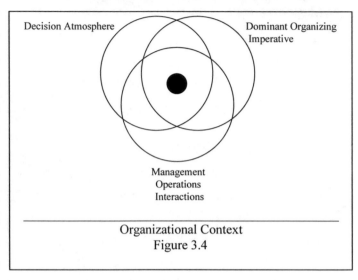

Decision Atmosphere

Dominant Organizing Imperative

Management Operations Interactions

Organizational Context
Figure 3.4

enterprise (e.g. marketing). People will be comfortable focusing on the overall goal and major milestones, and can be managed using these more effectively than with a detail task plan. However some projects will require more detail planning, especially if large, so extra effort will be needed by the project manager to sell this level of planning to the stakeholders (see Figure 3.4).

Organizational Image

When considering the context of a project it may be difficult to find an adequate way to describe it. Many important issues may be lost to awareness because they've become so ingrained in the way things are done and the assumptions about what is important. One way to identify an entire general context is to employ an image analysis. Images used in the past have been machines, brains, cultures, political systems, and even psychic prisons (Morgan, 1986). Rather than review each of these, it may be more meaningful to develop your own organizational image. A group of willing people with a history in the organization is needed. New employees aren't very helpful since they have little background to develop an accurate organizational image.

Most people find this exercise stimulating and pleasant. The analysis may be a bit tricky but can draw out facts about the enterprise that would normally remain hidden. Data used for the analysis is gathered from images people provide. An image can be provided by completing the following sentence:

The enterprise I work for is just like   _____.

The blank is filled in with the title of a book, movie, fairy tale, etc. Those providing the image also supply reasons for why a particular image comes to mind. For instance if the image was the book *Moby Dick*, reasons could be the enterprise is challenging and doggedly pursues its goals. As the person who will analyze the images generated by this exercise you may want to restrict the images to those you are familiar with since connections between the various images are easier to see. The process continues by collecting and combining them into a comprehensive image for the entire enterprise. This comprehensive image can be used to provide a rich contextual meaning for how and why decisions in and around your project are made, and how the project might be managed more effectively. The evaluation of the images is done using *grounded theory*. It's a way to lift implications from the information provided. "A *grounded theory* is one that's inductively derived from the study of the phenomenon." (Strauss, 1990). The process consist of a series of steps outlined below and summarized in Figure 3.5:

1. Data gathering: Ask the image question along with a request for why the image seems to fit the enterprise. Ideally this should be written down so you can evaluate it off-line. Some people may only talk about their image, and if that is the case, you need to take careful and detailed notes of what is said. It is not appropriate to question the image provider but to simply record the information. It's important to make sure everyone who is providing an image is speaking about the same enterprise or the same part of the enterprise – make sure the boundary is the same for everyone. You could do this just for your own work group or department if it is large enough. Ten to fifteen people should provide images.

2. Open coding: Collect all the images and read through them looking for key concepts and collect these together within various groups. Build on the concepts

where it seems reasonable. You may add items to test the description for robustness and accuracy. These additions are based on your work to integrate the various images.

3. Check: Go back to the originator of the image and see if your remodeling and concepts make sense and that they agree with what was provided. Ask for additions and integrate them into the existing individual analysis. Be careful not to "lead the witness".

4. Axial coding: Identify independent dimensions using statements and concepts that cut across most or all of the images. Look for interactions between images and within images that provide additional insight. New concepts may arise that could now be included.

5. Check: Provide a brief written account of all the images to the originators along with the concepts that they elicited. Test to see if the concepts are independent of one another, or how they might be dependent on one another.

6. Take into account the feedback in step five and develop an overall description of the enterprise.

See Appendix E for an example of a collection of images drawn from one enterprise and analyzed using the *grounded theory* approach.

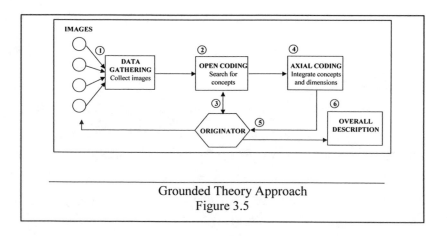

Grounded Theory Approach
Figure 3.5

An organizational image can reduce confusion on how to manage projects, just as knowing someone's personality will go a long way toward knowing how best to communicate with them, and how to approach them with questions and solutions. An image can also reveal the culture of an enterprise, where culture is the taken for granted notion of how people collaborate to get their work done, and survive in their external environment / market (Schein, 1985). Image brings into awareness the off-conscious assumptions about what the enterprise really values. Knowing these values may go a long way toward understanding and effectively dealing with organizational policies and key project enterprise stakeholders (Delisi, 1990).

Two questions are worth considering in applying the organizational image:

1. Does the project fit the image?

2. Does the way the project is carried out fit the image?

For question one a brief description of the project is needed concentrating on the project's objectives(s). From this description a word or two should be used to represent the project. Does the project support or not support the organizational image. Figure 3.6 provides possible project images. Question two reveals possible project process issues that may arise during project execution. Once again one or two words should be used to represent the process of project (see Figure 3.7).

Shooting star Train wreck Pillow Mule train Speedboat Bullet Yoyo Baby stroller ——————— Project Image Words Figure 3.6

Glider Ice skating Sword Semi truck Heart bypass Bacteria Slalom Roulette ——————— Project Process Words Figure 3.7

Understanding the context within which a project exists is critical for being able to manage it. Context sets the foundation for how decisions impact project performance, how people will view the project and hence support or not support it, as well as how the project team interprets its identity within a larger world.

Chapter 4

Project Aspects (Types)

It's amazing how one type of musical instrument is so much harder to play than another. It may take much determination and practice to get a note out of a saxophone that doesn't sound like a duck with gastritis, or a pleasant note from a violin that goes well beyond an amplified version of fingernails on the blackboard. The piano is a different story. One push on any key and you're as good at that note as Frederick Chopin (so to speak). Projects are like that. Some types of projects are easier to play (manage) than others. Looking at just a few aspects of a project can reveal its type, as well as how risky it might be.

By thinking of projects in broad terms one can identify certain aspects that make one kind of project different than another – or a way to classify them into types. After a series of interviews one researcher identified three critical aspects of projects that make them different; and depending on these aspects, the projects should be managed differently (McFarlan, 1981). Aspects are early indicators useful for determining project actions. Aspects include the project *size*, its *structure*, and its *technology*. While such distinctions are very subjective, and context dependent; they provide an initial insight into how to manage the project. These aspects are also a good way to assess the relative risk of a project. Also, in the parametric approach, identifying a type of project is one way to determine the relevancy of other parameters for managing projects (which parameters should be "in play").

Developing Baseline Project Portfolio

There are two possible measures for each of the three aspects of *size, structure,* and *technology.* – size would be large or small, structure high or low, and technology high or low. A project's *size* is determined by its relative position with other projects within the same enterprise. What may be large for one enterprise may not be for another. Size should be considered on several dimensions. These include how much time is required to complete the project (its duration), how many people are involved (including the team and stakeholders), the budget, and how many other areas within the enterprise will be impacted (the project's reach).

Structure of a project is how much is known about the deliverable(s) when the project begins. If the requirements are clear the project is high *structure*, or at least has the potential to be highly structured. If the requirements or deliverables(s) of the project are ill-defined the project is low *structure*.

The *technology* a project requires to manage it, to produce the deliverable, and even to be embedded in the deliverable itself has an impact on how the project should be managed. A high technology project will be more difficult to manage than one that is relatively technologically simple. *Technology* also depends upon a particular enterprise's ability. What may be high tech for one may not be for another (see Figure 4.1). Figure 4.2 shows the eight types of projects as identified by their aspects.

Aspect	Indicated Value	Key Elements
Size	Large, Small	Duration, People, Budget, Reach Enterprise-relevant
Structure	High, Low	Knowledge of project Deliverable clarity
Technology	High, Low	Management, Production, Deliverable Enterprise-relevant

Project Aspects and Values
Figure 4.1

Aspect values should be identified within a baseline of understanding for the enterprise. This can be accomplish through a rigorous process of deciding from previous projects what constitutes large/small *size*, high/low *structure*, and high/low *technology*. An implied baseline is present when people making assessments have a significant history or background with the enterprise.

		Structure			
		High	Low		
Technology	Low	1	5	Large	Size
		2	6	Small	
	High	3	7	Large	
		4	8	Small	

Eight Project Types
Figure 4.2

Project Risk

The three aspects of *size, structure* and *technology* can be used to assess the relative riskiness of an individual project or for an entire portfolio of projects. The most and least risky project types are evident from the three aspects. Large, low *structure* and high *technology* projects are the most risky, while small, high *structure* and low *technology* are the least risky. Deciding the next most/least risky requires additional reasoning around *structure* and *technology*. For most instances technology issues can be addressed by hiring, contracting, or education. If time is short hiring consultants with appropriate technology backgrounds may prove useful. However its hard to reduce risk for projects with low structure (those with unclear requirements or deliverable specificity) since the possibilities for the desired outcome of the project could almost be infinite. Therefore the next most risky project is large, low *structure* and low *technology*, and the next least risky would be small, high *structure*, and high *technology* (see Figure 4.3).

		Project Type Description	Type Number
Risk	High	Large, Low Structure, High Tech	7
		Large, Low Structure, Low Tech	5
	Medium	Large, High Structure, High Tech	3
		Large, High Structure, Low Tech	1
		Small, Low Structure, High Tech	8
		Small, Low Structure, Low Tech	6
	Low	Small, High Structure, High Tech	4
		Small, High Structure, Low Tech	2

Project Type Risks
Figure 4.3

Some enterprises may desire a certain risk factor for their project portfolio. This is related to the speed of innovations within their industry or environment. If they need to compete at a high rate of innovation a more risky portfolio may be needed than if they don't. When the desired riskiness of the portfolio is not what it should be, a risk assessment of each project may be needed to see if it fits with the planned risk profile. The percentages of planned and actual risks of a portfolio can be used to see if the current project fits within the planned risk profile (see Figure 4.4).

	Risk Profile		
	High	Medium	Low
Plan	30%	45%	25%
Actual	10%	50%	40%

Risk Profile of Project Portfolio
Figure 4.4

Figure 4.4 shows a situation where high risk projects would be more appealing and more likely to get approved (provided the project is within the boundary of reason).

Management Action/Devices Categories

The three measures for *size, structure*, and *technology* provide information to develop an approach on how the project should be managed. Four managerial action categories are possible: *Internal integration, external integration, formal planning*, and *formal control*. Each of these is more or less important depending on the type of project.

External integration is communicating across the project boundary into outside stakeholder arenas. This could be general management, the eventual users, or even suppliers. The way to cross this boundary is using devices that bring these outside influences into the awareness of those participating directly on the project. These devices include, but are not limited to those shown in Figure 4.5. External integration usually involves some sort of formal communication plan with key stakeholders.

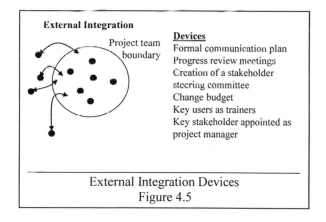

External Integration Devices
Figure 4.5

Internal integration is about bringing the project team together in closer communication and harmony. Key to this is to recognize who is really a part of the project and how their contribution should be measured by itself and in conjunction with others. Role clarity is key along with a willingness to interact across roles within the project team. Non-performers must be dealt with or disintegration will occur. While there are many approaches to achieving internal integration some are listed in Figure 4.6. Additional ideas can be found in chapter 7 on teams.

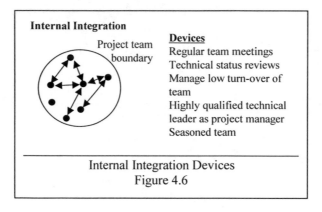

Internal Integration Devices
Figure 4.6

Formal planning is a process that takes place before the project is either approved or work begins. There are two formal plans worth considering. One is the formal plan used for approval, and the other is a plan that will get "worked". This may sound like sacrilege but it is closer to what actually happens than the myth of a single plan.

Many would-be project managers produce a plan that is unacceptable and tweak the numbers so that it becomes acceptable. Between the initial proposal and the subsequent plan, nothing usually changes. The scope remains the same, the number of people are the same (or less in some cases), and the time frame is the same (or shorted in most cases). To take this plan into the project and pretend it is the one to use to manage the project is truly living a lie. The approved plan may be the one that has to be reported against, but should not be the one used to actually manage the project. If an individual wants to be successful as a project manager, then, "to thine own self be true", is a good planning motto. Formal planning is required on projects that have substantial time or budgets involved. Usually the more formal the more detail is used. At the most detail level each individual task is identified and the tasks are related together in formal ways. Multiple estimates for each project task may be required (see PERT in chapter 8). The major issue is to develop a model of how the project will unfold, and in a form that will communicate the appropriate level of detail to all the stakeholders. Not every project should go through a formal planning process. See Figure 4.7 for examples of formal planning devices, and chapter 8, Planning Techniques.

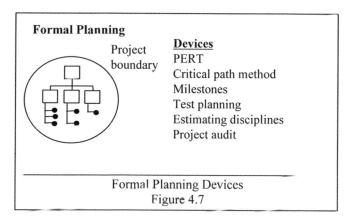

Formal Planning Devices
Figure 4.7

Project control is all about monitoring the plan against what's actually happening once the project begins to make sure it's within guidelines. There are four ways to control a project: one is at the task level and is the most detail and time-intensive approach, but it's the approach to use when the least amount of variance is desired. The second level of control is by milestone. The tasks scheduled between milestones are not monitored, but constant awareness of when milestones are occurring and communicating this across all stakeholders is important. The third way of controlling a project is outside control. People outside the project workgroup may have more to do with how the project actually unfolds than those within the group. This way of controlling can be accomplished through change budgets and disciplines usually focusing on schedule and cost. Controlling a project at the task level subsumes the other levels, and controlling at the milestone subsumes the change budget level. The forth level of control is almost no control at all. It's usually accomplished through infrequent stakeholder meetings, and the project managers interacting on a personal level with the project team (see chapter 9 for more details).

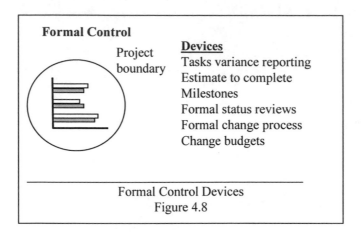

Formal Control Devices
Figure 4.8

Task level control means breaking up the project into manageable and meaningful tasks that represent time frames, which lend themselves to adjustment and rescheduling. The rule of thumb is each task should be estimated no more than 40 hours (or 5 days). The idea is that each task, if small enough, and is not completed as scheduled; an early enough warning is provided that an adjustment can be performed. It may take a year to build a good web site, but if you want to know how things are going during its construction so adjustments can be made, then more detail is needed and individual tasks should be identified and estimated for completion with 5 or less days each. While this needs to occur within the planning stage, during project execution is when it really pays off. It brings the project under more possible control. Remember not all project are controllable at a detail level. It depends on their type (among other things). Control devices are shown in Figure 4.8.

How much and what kind of devices are used have a relationship with the three measurements (*size, structure*, and *technology*) of the type of project. *Size* is more critical for deciding the device of *formal planning* and *formal control*. *Size* has a first order relationship with these devices (see Figure 4.9 below). There may be second order management considerations for an *aspect* and they are presented below as well. As first order considerations: If a project is large it requires planning and control. If it has low *structure* it requires a lot of external integration in order to bridge the gap between what is unknown by the project team with what is accepted by external stakeholders if the project is a high technology project then a lot of *internal integration* is needed. *Internal integration* is about getting the team together in order to share knowledge about the technology as the project unfolds (see Figure 4.9).

Project Measure	Management Devices Needed			
	External Integration	Internal Integration	Formal Planning	Formal Control
Size (large)			√	√
Low Structure	√			
High Tech		√		

First Order Relationships with Management Devices
Figure 4.9

Now that first order managerial considerations have been identified, its worth looking into second order relationships. If a project is very small it's not worth the time investment to plan it in detail or to establish tight controls. It would be easier to just get it done and not waste a lot of time planning it. If the project is of low *structure* then it does not lend itself to planning but still could be controlled through good stakeholder interaction. If the project is high tech then it does not lend itself to planning. With high tech the technology is such an unknown that making elaborate plans is usually fruitless – every day may bring project surprises that could not be anticipated by a detail plan (see Figure 4.10)

Project Measure	Management Devices Needed			
	External Integration	Internal Integration	Formal Planning	Formal Control
Size (small)			No-√	No-√
Low Structure			No-√	√
High Tech			No-√	

Second Order Relationships with Management Devices
Figure 4.10

By combining first and second order relationships there is an overall relationship to managing devices and the type of project. This is shown in Figure 4.11.

Type	Project Measures	Management Devices Needed			
		External Integration	Internal Integration	Formal Planning	Formal Control
1	High structure, low tech, large	Low	Medium	High	High
2	High structure, low tech, small	Low	Low	Medium	High
3	High structure, high tech, large	Low	High	Medium	Medium
4	High structure, high tech, small	Low	High	Low	Low
5	Low structure, low tech, large	High	Medium	High	High
6	Low structure, low tech, small	High	Low	Medium	High
7	Low structure, high tech, large	High	High	Low+	Low+
8	Low structure, high tech, small	High	High	Low	Low

Project Type and Management Devices Relationships
Figure 4.11

Summary

It's important to have a way to assess projects before they are planned where a lot of energy could be expended living up to an ascribed method, or series of managerial devices, when these devices may not fit the project. By using the three aspects of *size, structure* and *technology*, a project manager can assess a project and then plan for which devices should be employed. In the parametric analysis approach this is a primary parameter since it can be used to show relevancy of some of the other secondary parameters. For example, if the *size* of a project is large, *formal planning*, a secondary parameter should be seriously considered.

Projects of Life – The Wedding

There are huge differences on how weddings take place. There's the quick trip to Las Vegas, a visit to a commercial wedding chapel, and snap it's done – off to the honeymoon (or gaming tables). Some weddings are so large and complex that a wedding planner is needed to arrange all the details. A cast of people is needed to pull it off. This large wedding project will require planning. Traditional weddings lend themselves to planning since they are a well understood series of tasks. Planning traditional weddings can prove to be very beneficial and go a long way to satisfy all the major stakeholders (e.g. the wedding couple, the parents, and guests).

Changing the wedding project aspects from a large, highly structured traditional wedding to an inventive/innovative wedding changes the need for planning. Suppose the wedding is an elopement, conducted by a justice of the peace somewhere between home and a nice hotel room. A lot of planning would be almost useless – for small, low structure, and innovative projects, planning should be minimal. Some planning is always needed –gas up the car, get a ladder to reach her bedroom window, pack for the trip etc.

Planning a wedding at the individual task level is quite possible. Relationships between the tasks will be important. Some tasks will take place at the same time (e.g. seating of the guests while the appropriate wedding music is being performed), while other tasks have strong dependencies (e.g. the loud bridal march music does not begin until the bride is ready to walk down the aisle). One could draw a network diagram of all the tasks that need to take place in a wedding. Included in these tasks could be milestones in the wedding such as when to start the bridal march, when to introduce the bride and groom as wedded, and when to dismiss the guests.

The master wedding planner doesn't need to draw a network diagram if he/she has sufficient wedding experience and has, for the most part, memorized all the steps and dependencies. To master a project the project manager may have to physically create a network diagram to internalize it. Internalizing a project, getting it firmly in one's mind, can make decision and changes easier to manage. Internalization is a job that cannot be handed off to another since through this process understanding the project takes place.

Projects of Life – The Wedding (continued)

The weddings described above do not take into account the many differences between cultures and religions found throughout the world. While some weddings are like others, every one is unique and needs someone to manage the process.

PART THREE

Organization Issues

A project requires organization in order for it to be reasonably successful. This is a similar issue as *context* reviewed earlier, but the following chapters deal with carrying out the project through an organized problem and people approach.

A project can be described as an organization of activities set in place trying to accomplish a goal. Another way to look at it is as a problem that needs a solution. The problem can be characterized in various ways independent of its particular solution. This can be done using a generalized problem-solving model resulting in the three problem orientations of *monolithic, incremental*, and *evolutionary*.

Another organizational consideration is the structure of the innovation-based department. Does everyone report to the same boss (extremely flat) or is there a hierarchy of reporting relationships that needs to be considered? Four organizational styles are examined.

Projects are often accomplished through a team effort and these teams will need to be organized in some fashion to be productive. Team formation and team structure are two variants of the parameter of *team* within the concept of project management. These two approaches to team organization are examined. Team formation is about how to get a team organized or built so that it can eventually be productive. Team structure is about the relationships and roles, both formal and informal, between project team members. Four possible team structures are presented.

Chapter 5

Problem Orientation

The car is packed, coffee mugs hot and filled, the road is clear, and you and your significant other are headed for a nice vacation trip to a neighboring state. It's not long after crossing the border an argument ensues. Your partner wants to stop at the next town because billboard ads about unique shops and sites make it very appealing. However, this stop is not in your plan, and if taken means skipping some of the planned activities. You've planned the trip as a linear monolithic process while your partner assumes the trip is about evolutionary exploration of new opportunities and sites. In this example each person has their own orientation to "the problem" of visiting a neighboring state revealing that problems can be solved in more than one way – and not always contributing to harmonious bliss.

Life can be viewed as a series of solutions to simple, difficult, and even complex problems. How people solve these problems is reflected in their background, dispositions, and styles. Some may flip a coin or even "just the problem solve itself", others may document the problem and seek advice from friends and family, and still others may pray and seek spiritual guidance. Each of these represents how one orients themselves to the problems that face them. Projects face the major problem of producing a deliverable. But rather than depend on individual whimsical approaches for producing the deliverable three orientations are suggested – *monolithic, incremental*, and *evolutionary*.

Just as there's more than one way to skin a cat, there's more than one way to produce the major deliverable of a project. One reason projects are so difficult to manage is the lack of understanding about the variety of management approaches, and when one would be better than another. Equifinality in systems thinking reveals that for an open system there's the potential for arriving at a solution from many pathways (von Bertalanffy, 1981). Projects are open systems and deliverable production is an equifinal problem. Limiting possible solution paths to three reduces the complexity and confusion surrounding deliverable creation. These three paths are derived from the problem solving model of Nobel laureate Herbert Simon (Simon, 1977). Also, knowing the relative strengths and weaknesses of the three paths or orientations provides additional insight on how to manage the project (see Figure 5.1). This generalized model is used to solve problems from every possible domain of knowledge or specialization – from designing and making an automobile, to creating automated information systems within an enterprise.

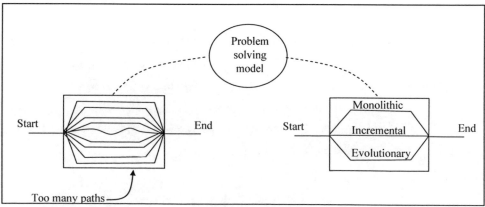

Equifinality of Projects

Figure 5.1

A problem orientation is an approach on how to produce the major deliverable of a project, not how to manage the project. The project manager should be knowledgeable about these approaches but not overemphasize them resulting in inattention to all the other issues (parameters) needed to manage a project.

Generalized Problem Solving Model

The general model consists of five steps. Step one is gathering information, or intelligence about the problem under consideration. Step two, is analyzing the information gathered, step three designing alternative solutions, step four, choosing which alterative is best (or how to arrange all the alternatives), and step five, obtaining feedback to the previous steps for reconsideration (see Figures 5.2 and 5.3). Figure 5.3 shows emphasis for each of the three orientations. *Monolithic* emphasizes a single time through the process with little or no feedback, while *incremental* emphasizes design and choosing (or aligning) alternatives/parts, and *evolutionary* emphasizes feedback steps. Depending on the problem, and the skill of those "solving" it, the process will unfold differently.

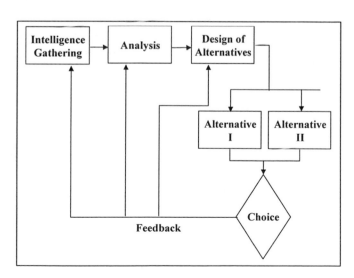

General Problem Solving Approach
Figure 5.2

Steps	Solution Approach		
	Monolithic	Incremental	Evolutionary
1. Intelligence Gathering	X	--	--
2. Analysis	X	--	--
3. Design	X	X	--
4. Choosing	X	X	--
5. Feedback		--	X
	Once	**Divisions**	**Repeatedly**

Problem Solving Emphasis For Approaches
Figure 5.3

Monolithic Approach

Proceeding through the process from intelligence gathering through choosing an alternative is considered the *monolithic* approach. No feedback to previous steps is provided, so each step should be carefully considered before moving on to the next. It's like taking on the problem as one big monolith such as building a large model airplane – following the instructions step by step and ending with the final product (the airplane).

This is a beginning-to-end strategy, emphasizing one time through the process. Few changes are either anticipated or wanted. The overall strategy is to solve the problem once by having all the intelligence to solve it up front. As the process unfolds each step is made with full knowledge from the last step. The approach is based on gathering all the intelligence up front, analyzing all this intelligence ruling out irrelevant items and connecting those that seem to fit together, designing several alternatives to the problem that present themselves from the analyzed intelligence, and then using well-known criteria to choose the best alternative and implementing that alternative.

With the *monolithic* orientation you have good trace-ability of items through the process, clear demarcations from one solution step to the next, usually good documentation due to the formality of the exchange between steps, a nicely integrated finished product, and a process usually understood by stakeholders. The *monolithic* approach lends itself to good documentation, and the skills required to accomplish each step are relatively clear. Steps are adjustable depending how much each will require based on the sort of problem being solved, and the capability of those participating. Adjustments to the *monolithic* approach are not complex and do not require a different way of understanding how the model works. The adjustments are a matter of which steps are emphasized within the project. For example if the intelligence or knowledge about the problem is already known, then this step should receive relatively little attention compared with other steps.

The *monolithic* approach has several limitations. There is no real deliverable or product until the end. During analysis, design, and implementation little contact with the major stakeholders is required. Presumably most of the contact is done during intelligence gathering (or requirements definition in some methods). So with this approach most of the work is being accomplished with accumulated costs when there is the least amount of contact with major stakeholders. This may not bode well on projects that go across funding cycles while major stakeholders are mostly uninvolved (money spent with "nothing" to show for it). The *monolithic* approach has a heavy outside communication demand on both the front and back end. On the front end the project manager needs to make sure the requirements are clear because there's no natural way for them to evolve over time, and on the back to make sure that what has been developed is understood well enough to be used, and the value of its usage is clear. Keeping stakeholders well informed during the entire *monolithic* process needs overt attention since little from the approach will provide it, and loss of support may result.

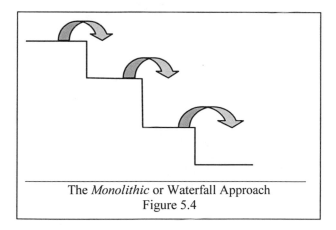

The *Monolithic* or Waterfall Approach
Figure 5.4

The biggest drawback to the *monolithic* approach is dealing with changes. Changes are heavily discouraged since it's a one-time-through process. While building a model airplane, if you've glued the fuselage pieces together as well as the pilot's canopy, it really is too late to put in the pilot seat you either forgot about or was missed in the instructions. Change control procedures are usually put into place during the project to stave off changes, or make sure the changes are really necessary to produce the final deliverable. One danger with this approach is that the final product may get delivered as promised, but not used because the needed changes weren't made due to an overly suppressive change control policy.

The *monolithic* approach is often called the waterfall model because when one step is completed the results are pushed along to the next step until the project has flowed over every step in the model like water over a series of steps. The information technology community often referred to the approach as the Systems Development Life Cycle or SDLC (Stair, 1999). See Figure 5.4.

Incremental Approach

This problem orientation is concerned with breaking up the whole problem into manageable pieces. The emphasis in the model is on construction of alternatives after the intelligence, analysis, and design are done (design is key). Alternatives may not be alternative solutions to the whole problem, but designed subdivisions of the problem to be worked out separately. Each alternative, or subdivision, if decoupled from one another can be worked on independently if desired. Some feedback is provided across subdivisions especially if they are not implemented at the same time. Each partial solution is not a cut-down version of the final product, but an operational deliverable that's a part of the total solution. An example would be building twenty-mile stretches of a highway between two cities a hundred miles apart. Each stretch would be an increment and usable before the total highway is completed. There may be some overhead up front to set up an environment that can incrementally accommodate additions to the total solution. Also, there may be some effort at the end to integrate the partial solutions.

The *incremental* approach has been referred to as the structured approach to problem solving (Yourdon, 1979). In essence you work on one part of the problem, solve it completely and stub-out the rest (hold the other parts as separate units). While building the model airplane we could enlist the aid of a colleague to assemble the landing gear while personally assembling the cockpit. Since they are stand-alone parts they can be worked on independently and then assembled later (see Figure 5.5).

The *incremental* approach is flexible due to the possibility of multiple branches. It also allows one to decouple the project – arranging project parts so each part basically stands alone. Other advantages of this approach includes cross-sharing between branches, balancing resources between branches, and providing a quicker solution to the overall problem provided there are sufficient resources to work on more than one branch at a time. The *incremental* approach presents an implied structure to the final deliverable that gets communicated simply by the structure. It's good for large projects because dividing a large project may make it more manageable than taking on the whole thing at once. For the *incremental* approach a deliverable is produced before the end if the project. Having a deliverable before the end will facilitate stakeholder awareness and support. While changes are discouraged some changes are possible between structural arms.

The biggest advantage of this approach is producing something that actually functions before the end of the entire project, and each increment can be used to influence the next increment. It's one way to build on previous successes and give the whole project a sense of forward progress in the minds of some key stakeholders. Unlike the *monolithic* you do not have to wait until the end to obtain value from the effort

Disadvantages to this approach include the need to pre-design the structure, provide integration of pieces at the end, coordinate between structures (especially if they are being worked concurrently), and to keep everyone focused on the main objective of the project rather than see the branch as representing competing objectives with the others. Another disadvantage with the *incremental* approach is that parts

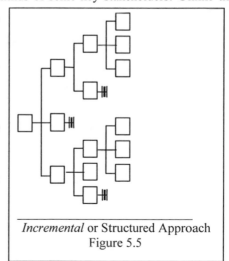

Incremental or Structured Approach
Figure 5.5

getting implemented early will have to be maintained even when new parts are being developed. This presents priority problems for the project manager – is maintenance of existing working pieces more important than development of the entire system? Maintenance often becomes a problem for the project manager in *incremental* projects since the whole project isn't officially turned over to a regular maintenance process until the project is completed (all parts are working).

Evolutionary Approach

The *evolutionary* orientation to solving problems concentrates on the feedback loop. This approach produces a mock-up or prototype of the system quickly to get reactions from major stakeholders. Usually a special tool is involved in building the prototype, and the result, while representing the complete system, is not useable as is. The prototype is built for reaction not for production. Three prototypes are usually appropriate to achieve a real workable result. With the model airplane example, the model could be a mock-up of a real airplane. It's a non-functioning representation of the actual end product. With information systems the prototype may not have a functioning database with real data, or may be lacking the kind of access to other required executable resources. It may lack the ability to be "ramped up" with the number of people who will eventually be using the system. Due to volume efficiencies the *evolutionary* project deliverable may be remade through a *monolithic* process (see Figure 5.6).

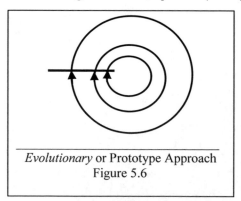

Evolutionary or Prototype Approach
Figure 5.6

Since feedback is critical to this approach, contact and communication with the target stakeholder group is integral to the process. Without a good communication relationship with this group the *evolutionary* approach should be avoided. When adequately set up, interfacing with the eventual user and constant feedback provide higher levels of stakeholder satisfaction because of the consistent attention throughout the process. Unlike the *monolithic* approach where attention is provided up-front during intelligence gathering or requirements definition, this approach fosters communication throughout the project. The *evolutionary* approach could be considered more informal and hence more reliant on personal relationships between major stakeholders and the project team. New employees are more difficult to work into this approach because of their lack of such relationships.

Advantages of the *evolutionary* approach include an early-on sense of the final product, continuing interaction, natural process for dealing with changes, and almost a self-documenting process where the product user learns the system as it evolves. The major advantage is discovery of the real operational requirements from those who will utilize the end product or major deliverable. Quick feedback will bring quick adjustments to match the needs of the target stakeholders.

There are a number of drawbacks to this *evolutionary* approach. These include too early acceptance, lack of discipline about what has already been accomplished, and knowing when you're done. The early buy-in could mean that the system may not have a chance to evolve, as it should. If the assumption is to let the product evolve, then stopping the evolution with the first version may mean it will never work appropriately. This happens because people may not have confidence in the process, and consider the first version better than anything they've had before and want to protect it. Hence they will not participate in its evolution. Also, the approach implies a lack of discipline that may produce an impression that always starting over is okay. The process then becomes a constant loop of refinement to initial thoughts rather than an evolution of thought toward a final product. Freezes will be required to alleviate this problem. Finally, the evolutions may never end. There is always room for improvement, and unless there is an official expected end to the project, the assumption may be made that it will continually evolve making the end of the project indefinable.

Once the project is officially over the major deliverable may evolve, but this evolution is not being managed as part of the original project. The evolutionary nature of project deliverables, both before and after implementation, has been studied (Orlikowski, 1996). The *evolutionary* approach is particularly appropriate when the project is complex and has integrative components, but is not large. Larger projects with these characteristics are more appropriately accomplished through an *incremental* approach where the project can be divided into manageable segments. However, even when projects are large, complex, and have a significant integrative nature, evolution will occur. This has been found to be true for Enterprise Resource Planning (ERP) systems. The evolution of these systems takes place once the system is implemented (or "goes live") (Diehl, 2003). Pre-implementation evolution can be expected on small, complex projects that have a strong integrative nature. These would be like many web-oriented application systems that become very visible to their major stakeholders during construction when changes are encouraged and implemented quickly but also will need to be integrated with back-office systems. Their post-implementation evolution should be low since their evolution occurred beforehand (see Figure 5.7).

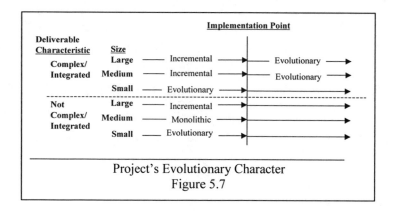

Project's Evolutionary Character
Figure 5.7

The Purchase Package Issue

In the information technology community sometimes rather than building solutions they are bought from already constructed solutions – some maybe a purchased package, others maybe Common Off The Shelf System (COTS). The talent and skills needed to purchase rather than build solutions are somewhat different. There are considerations for which model to utilize for COTS. If the purchased system covers the entire set of requirements, then an adjusted *monolithic* approach may be the best. Since it provides everything, the major issue is to confirm this and get the system installed. The approach should be *incremental* when there are parts missing, or if the purchase is made "one piece at a time" rather than as a whole package. Finally if the package is seen as an automated model of reality to be compared to the actual behavior-set for the enterprise, then the purchased package actually can be considered as an *evolutionary* prototype of what may eventually get built.

Memory Model explanation

Some people may find one of these approaches (*monolithic, incremental,* or *evolutionary*) more natural than the others. These people may get so good at their most natural approach the others might not get considered even if they are more appropriate for the project at hand. The talent to manage each of these three approaches can be viewed as a relative strength/weakness of one's ability to use memory appropriately. One memory model of how humans solve problems contains four parts. These are Short-Term Memory (STM), Long-Term Memory (LTM), external memory (EM), and the actual process of information manipulation. STM is where the manipulation takes place. Certain information is held in STM until it is no longer needed, then more information is recalled from LTM and/or EM into STM for usage. The amount of information that comes into and used by STM is said to be limited to seven plus or minus two "chunks" (Miller, 1956). The way we get better at solving problems is to be able to stuff more information into an information "chunk". The way information gets into LTM is through rehearsal and recall.

The point here is that each of the three problem solving approaches relies on varying uses of the parts of the memory model. The *monolithic* requires EM since all the information cannot be held in STM or LTM. The *monolithic* approach is strong in providing good documentation. The *incremental* approach combines the need for EM and LTM. While good documentation is possible with the *incremental* approach, one must remember the issues of integration associated with the *incremental* approach emphasizing LTM and STM. Also, the *incremental* approach is not as responsive as the *evolutionary*, but because of integration issues for *incremental* more STM is needed than for the *monolithic*. The *evolutionary* approach relies primary on STM to solve the problems in a quick responsive manner. STM's ability to increase the density of a "chunk" means the evolutionary approach can be used on more than trivial problems (see Figures 5.8 and 5.9).

Some people are better at using their memory in certain ways which suggests that the project manager should choose the problem orientation that best fits their memory strengths. However, projects usually come with a preferred orientation and the project manager needs to be able to adjust their memory approach. If one is used to managing projects with the evolutionary orientation (a sort of seat-of-the-pants approach), more skills will be needed for documentation and control in the other orientations which will require memory to be used differently – especially external memory. Memory strengths may become weaknesses as the project manager moves from one project to another.

Figure 5.10 shows a comparison of the three problem orientations across several characteristics of projects. Knowing the most beneficial orientation for your project will make it simpler to manage and maybe even finish when expected.

Approach	Memory Component			
	EM	LTM	STM	Probl. Solv. (Chunking)
Monolithic	High	Medium	Medium	Low
Incremental	Medium	High	Medium	Medium
Evolutionary	Low	Medium	High	High

Memory Emphasis by Approach
Figure 5.8

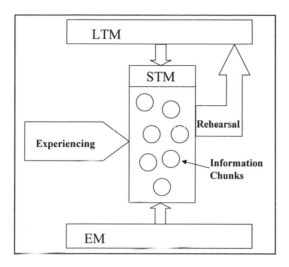

Memory Model
Figure 5.9

PROCESS	MONOLITHIC	INCREMENTAL	EVOLUTIONARY
ACTIVITIES	Consecutive	Concurrent	Iterative
INITIAL PRODUCT	Stand alone	Overlapped	Quick & Dirty
TECHNIQUES	Planned Total product "Sign-offs"	Parallel Expandable "Stubs"	Prototype Software support "Do-it-yourself" kits
PHASES	Baselines	Functions	Versions
CHANGES	Discouraged	Expected	Welcomed
MOTTO	"Freeze the specs"	"Add as permitted"	"Throw some away"
APPLICATIONS	Standard	Complex	Innovative Experimental
DURATION	Limited (6-9 months)	Expansive (over 12 months)	Quick (under 3 months)
END USERS	"Clients"	"Partners"	"Owners"
ORGANIZATION	Assembly line	Project team	Technical consultants
STRENGTH	Documentation	Visibility	Responsiveness

Comparison Between Problem Orientations
Figure 5.10

Chapter 6

Organizational Style/Structure

Ant farms are amazing to watch. It seems each ant is programmed with a behavior pattern that contributes to the greater good of the group. The standard, normal person has the capacity to change what they want based on a large variety of present and past circumstances and behaviors. Due to this human capacity, the achievement of a collective good needs explicit design. This explicit design is identified herein as organizational style. Enterprises that have high level skill requirements are often organized around these specialty skills. Other enterprises that deem projects vital to their survival/growth often arrange their people according to a pure project style. Further, enterprises that depend critically on knowledge of their products/services are often organized by these products/service domains of knowledge.

Enterprises are assembled to accomplish tasks reliability and repeatedly in hopes of achieving effective and efficient outcomes. Looking at enterprise organizational style is primarily a machine/process worldview where an organizational style is not concerned with individual people but with integrating tasks into an operational framework. Results of this analytic process are static structures representing the way things get done. While they carry the aura of facticity, the real organization remains one locked up into how, and through what channels, people really communicate (Barley, 1990). However, structures can function as a way to set up the needed communication, or simply as a way to relate expectations across a variety of people. In either case, operational structures have particular strengths and weaknesses when it comes to succeeding with a project.

Styles/Structures of Organizing

Four enterprise organizational forms are presented below. Information Technology (IT) and manufacturing will be used as examples of the styles. These four are *specialty functional, matrix, pure project*, and *application (or product)*. Organizational style, as used here, is not how teams are designed but how project resource assignments are made within an overall enterprise structure. How projects are lead and the role leaders play within the context of the enterprise is covered along with how each style addresses various project management features.

Consider a factory and its organization. One common way to organize a factory is by the products it produces. If the enterprise is manufacturing compressors and hydraulic tools, the factory may organize a section to make large compressors, another section for portable compressors, and one for hand tools. Each section of the factory has its own set of machines dedicated to that section's product. Here is a *product* (or *application* as we shall see later) style of organizing. After some consideration it may be more advantageous to organize around the sort of machines employed so more expertise for each machine (or technology) can grow. This is a *specialty* organizational style.

Specialty Functional Style/Structure (weak matrix)

In this style the enterprise may be organized in areas of functional specialization. Using manufacturing as a basis these units could include department functional specialties such as design, testing, plant layout, and process (where even the processes are arranged by machines needed for production as in the example above). So a project producing a new product would be managed through these specialties (see Figure 6.1). This specialization idea can also be applied on an information technology basis thus producing a *specialty functional* organizational style where producing a new information system is managed through IT specialties (see Figure 6.2).

For the IT example, projects are assigned to a project manager, often coming from the analytic or design arm, who is responsible for ushering the project through the IT specialties

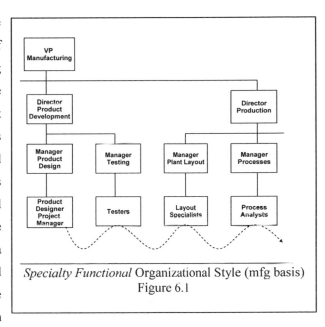

Specialty Functional Organizational Style (mfg basis)
Figure 6.1

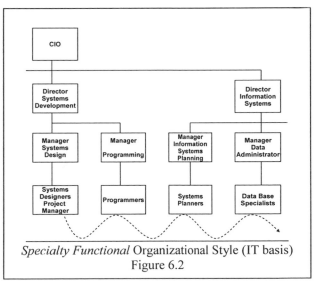

Specialty Functional Organizational Style (IT basis)
Figure 6.2

required. Within these specialties people work on tasks within a project as directed by their specialty management, and these people are not formally assigned to any project. As far as the project goes, the people are part of specialty pools that the project manager draws on when needed. There is no guarantee that the same people would be assigned throughout the life of the project. Work is assigned on an individual basis with little or no consideration for which project tasks belong. While negotiating with specialty department heads by the project manager is possible, the project manager has no formal authority to request specific people.

A rationale for this style is for efficient usage of specialists across all projects. Project managers are relieved from formal reporting and evaluations of people, but still have to ensure they are performing on the project according to plan. Project managers spend most of their time coordinating and communicating with the specialty areas to make sure proper attention is given to the project. Project managers may need to negotiate with one another at times to free resources during critical times. The project should be planned in as much detail as possible and modularized to accommodate multiple people working on the same deliverable. Also an emphasis on planning will help in the overall coordination of resources and provide early warning signals when more people may be needed.

Matrix Style/Structure (strong matrix)

The word matrix has many meanings and conjures up a variety of images. These may include long black-coated heroes from the movie "The Matrix", to those exciting days in math class where a matrix transformation was amazingly performed. In the case of enterprise organizational style, *matrix* is a way for people to be assigned to various projects and still maintain a "home" specialty base – the person is working in two organizational dimensions, hence the term matrix.

The attraction of a *matrix* style of organizing has an interesting history. Several decades ago *matrix* management was the new way of thinking about how to organize, and many management gurus were espousing it as the way to effectively and efficiently manage people and accomplish work. What resulted was a fast track into fiasco land. Shortcuts were taken for educating what matrix management was about, and it was applied as a "magic bullet" solution to many problems. The other big downfall was lack of tools to make it really effective. Today, tools such as email, distance/virtual meetings, and collaborative decision software are available to assist a *matrix* management style. After a time, the matrix approach fell into disrepute, but it has recently become more popular and viable. Still, many people will shutter at the notion of a *matrix* organization style due to its previous failures.

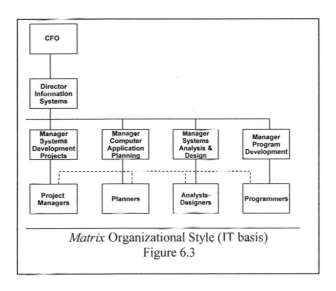

Matrix Organizational Style (IT basis)
Figure 6.3

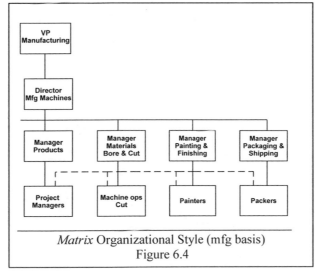

Matrix Organizational Style (mfg basis)
Figure 6.4

Running a project in an enterprise that uses the *matrix* style means individuals will more than likely be assigned to multiple projects at once while working out of a technology specialty pool (see Figures 6.3 and 6.4). This style is different that the *specialty functional* style because with the *matrix* people are formally assigned to a project or projects and work on many tasks within their assigned project(s). In *specialty* each task gets assigned independent of previous or future tasks. No project consistency for individuals is required or expected. For *matrix* individuals are purposefully assigned to a variety of tasks on the same project thus increasing project specific knowledge (this increase is not as much as in *pure project* as seen below). With the *matrix* style people have two or more bosses, but the project environment is still more consistent than with a *specialty functional* style (see Figure 6.5).

SPECIALIZATIONS	PROJECTS			
	A	B	C	D
Analysts	Joe, Mike	Mike	Joe	Joe
Programming	Sue	David	David	Mary Jerry
Database	Rich Donna	Donna	Ann	
Telecommunications	Jack		John Fanny	John
Maintenance/ Operations	Glen Larry	Larry		Larry

Matrix Assignments (IT basis)
Figure 6.5

As a project manager in a *matrix* style the major issue is to maintain attention on your project from its various technical contributors. Attention will usually be required for negotiating people time with other project managers. Also, the project will need to be planned in a way that tasks do not require long-term commitment by the people working on them. Individuals will be faced with balancing workloads between their projects, and if one task demands all of their time over long period, other projects may suffer along with the project manager's reputation that assigned the "mother-of-all" tasks. However, a balance will need to be struck during planning between dividing tasks into their lowest level of disaggregation, to overly aggressive expectations of time commitment to any one task. Reducing each task to its lowest level may result in too much wasted time in starting/stopping the work. Once a task is halted it may mean you will lose the attention for that project at the cost of working on another. Having small-disaggregated tasks means lots more negotiation as well as start/stop reduction in productivity. Cross-coordination between projects is a key to success for the *matrix* style. Not only are the modern computing and communication tools valuable for those accomplishing project work, they provide critical assistance for communicating across projects to establish optimal working timeframes by those performing on the project.

The *matrix* orientation will provide cross-project sharing of ideas so that work will not be isolated into business or technology silos. The *matrix* style accommodates varying demands for the number of people required during a project, and hence lends itself to an overall leveling of the people resource demand for all projects within the enterprise. While split loyalties are experienced in the *matrix* style, people will have a continuous flow of work resulting in a more efficient usage across the specialties since their down time can be managed better.

Pure Project Style/Structure

This organizational style is attractive to most project managers because there's little confusion on who is actually assigned to the project. Project workers are officially assigned to the project for its duration, and have one boss – the project manager. Negotiation between other projects is reduced or eliminated and the project manager has flexibility within the project for scheduling people. *Pure project* styles are a classic command structure with formal control held by the project manager. Organization for the project can be optimized for overall project effectiveness independent of what other things may be going on in other projects. If the project is large, subdividing it may be wise in order to distribute resources effectively and make it clear where elements of work belong. Project issue resolution can be accommodated by organizing the project to make it clear where and who should be performing project parts. The line outside the project manager's door may never go down if the project is not organized in a way that makes it clear who's responsible for accomplishing what parts of the project. As issues emerge on the project, a clear structure communicates where the issue should be addressed (see Figure 6.6).

One thing about this style is that it fosters personal identity to the project. Project identity is a two-edged sword, but if handled right can go a long way toward producing desired results. The project manager can facilitate a positive identity to the project by celebrating early "wins" within the project team. The more identity that forms the harder it will be emotionally on the project team as the project nears conclusion. People will begin to suffer some psychological distance with other team members if identity has been strong. When the project team is disbanded the strong project identity may result in a loss of motivation for individuals until the next great challenge is available and a new project identity formed. With the synergistic nature of the project lost the major deliverable of the project may receive inadequate attention by those who remain on the project for its "installation" (Kidder, 1981).

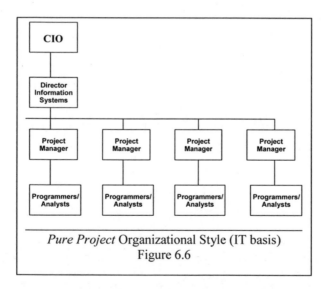

Pure Project Organizational Style (IT basis)
Figure 6.6

Individuals may suffer from disenchantment that comes when a great goal has been met, and no other great goal immediately presents itself. If you have been successful as a project manager and have built a high functioning team, then what will they do next? It may not be the project manager's problem, but then again within this style people may eventually become calloused to forming identities to projects thus losing the close working harmony and communication effectiveness characteristic of this organizational style.

Toward the end of the project the project team members will be wondering what their next project might be. They may spend more time and effort nailing down their next assignment than actually completing work on the existing assignment. In the worst case people may jump ship early in order to land on their next project.

The biggest challenge for a project manager under this style is to make sure the team is heading in the right direction. Team members will tend to identify strongly with the project since it is their primary work goal, however the project may end up with a life of its own, substituting a form of project identity and team cohesion, for meeting expected project deliverables. The project details and the people working on it may become more important in their minds than accomplishing the goal.

Application (Product) Style/Structure

When organized according to application, or business knowledge domain, each major application area has an Information Technology (IT) group assigned to it from within the IT area. (Also, see previous manufacturing example where the factory is organized by product.) When an IT project in an application area is approved it's assigned to that area's IT group. These areas could include engineering systems, marketing systems, manufacturing systems, etc. Because the arrangement is by application the tie between people in these application areas

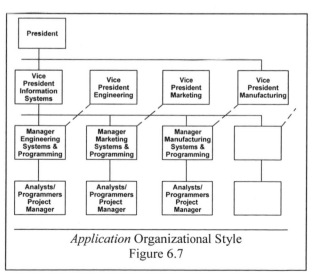

Application Organizational Style
Figure 6.7

and the IT support unit for each area should be strong. Knowledge of the application area within that area's IT group grows over time (see Figure 6.7).

An organization of this kind makes it simple to assign specific projects if they are non-integrative in nature. But for those large integrative projects such as Enterprise Resource Planning systems or highly integrated products that cross domain knowledge areas (such as wireless PDAs), the *application* organization style is not ideal. While fostering application knowledge this organization style does not lend itself to technology knowledge growth, nor to those projects that require integration across application areas.

People sharing a history of working together over time will develop an implicit way of conducting business which may not be evident to outsiders or new hires. It will take these people a while to know the ropes since some of the ropes are not even evident to current players. The assumptions by which people work have become "off-conscious" and lost from everyday awareness (Schein, 1985). So in the *application* style explicit ways to accommodate new people into the area is needed to overcome the social barrier usually present when people have worked together over a long period.

The *application* style provides a quick start up for most projects because people already know their roles, and much of the required area knowledge for the project may have already been learned from previous efforts. Also, many details about how things are done on projects have already been learned and in-grained through a history of shared experiences by the people who have been supporting the area over many years. As a

Organizational Style	Major Leadership Challenges
Specialist Functional	Communication and coordination between specializations and project workers.
Matrix	Cross project coordination with other project managers, and effective task planning for optimal resource sharing.
Pure project	Maintaining the project objective in the minds of all those participating, especially for those officially assigned to the project. Reduce the tendency for the project to take on a life of its own.
Application	Integrating project deliverables with other areas that may be affected. Accommodating new people into the area, and informal starts.

Major Project Leadership Challenges by Organizational Style
Figure 6.8

downside to this style system specifications may be shared in informal ways and in an attempt to be responsive to requesters the IT people may begin working on projects before their official approval. Also, it is more difficult to grow technically with this style since its emphasis is on application domain knowledge rather than technical knowledge (see Figure 6.8)

Organizational styles will have effects on various features of a project. These features include the clarity of project leadership (how well people understand who's actually leading the project), how information is shared between various projects, how information is shared across areas if the business, specialization development, the kind of *authority* that would prove most useful, individuals' identity to the project itself, job security from project to project, the timeliness for getting a project started, and the kind of intelligence the style engenders. See Figure 6.9 for a comparison of organizational styles across other project features.

	Organizational Style			
Feature	**Spec Functional**	**Matrix**	**Pure Project**	**Application**
Leadership Clarity	Informal (none)	Many leaders	One	One
Cross project sharing	Some	Much	None	Some
Cross Area Sharing	Some	Some	None	None
Tech. Specialization	Much	Much	Little	Little
Authority	Technical Bureaucratic	Charismatic Technical	Formal Charismatic	Bureaucratic Purse String
Project Identity	None	Some	Much	Some
Job Security	Some	Much	None	Much
Start up	Quick	Moderate	Slow	Quick
Intelligence	Technical	Balanced	Project	Domain

Features of Organizational Styles
Figure 6.9

Enterprises also have created organizations to establish and provide direction for project management functions. These have been labeled in various ways including the Project Management Office (PMO). The overall contribution of the discipline of project management to the enterprise suggests differing levels of importance spanning across strategic, tactical, and operational.

Strategic Project Management (PMO for mastery)

When project management is critical to the enterprise a deep level of skill is needed suggesting a project management mastery approach (see chapter 1). Project management is strategic if the enterprise product is tightly connected to managing projects, such as large scale construction, or if continual enterprise transformation is needed to remain competitive or able to deliver on the major mission. Project management masters are needed because too much depends on successful outcomes for projects.

In order to master project management one needs to start with a basic set of knowledge about what is required to manage projects. One also needs to be able to use the knowledge, and practice with the knowledge in ways that are separate from actual project performance. Also needed are ways to build more knowledge, practice to develop recognized expertise, and build meaning into being a master project manager. This can be achieved through a community of practice (CoP). And finally, the mastery capability needs to be deployed through a community of practice within the enterprise. Four critical steps toward achieving project management mastery are shown in Figure 6.10

1. Acquire a set of knowledge that embodies the notion of project management that can be built upon.
2. Be able to use the knowledge to practice project management separate from actually managing a real project.
3. Participate in an on-going group that is dedicated toward project management mastery such as a CoP.
4. Get individual enterprises on-board with the idea. A CoP is carried out at multiple levels the enterprise level being critical.

Mastery Development Steps
Figure 6.10

If the PMO is the organizational unit charged with building mastery then it will be involved in enterprise-wide decisions on education, qualifications, and credentials.

Tactical Project Management (PMO for control)

For some enterprises projects are not critical or strategic. Projects may be tactical because they're used to remodel current practices or reformulate current business connections and/or relationships. A PMO can provide control mechanisms so projects are consistently monitored and reported upon. It may also provide recommended procedures and methods for producing the project's major deliverable. They may also contribute to project priority setting as well as assist in stakeholder communication.

Operational Project Management (PMO for assistance)

Projects can be limited to providing operational efficiencies and ways to tie the enterprise together for small incremental improvements over time. For these enterprises no major changes are expected either internal or external to their primary mission. The PMO provides assistance and help for project managers usually involving tool usage, methodology training, enterprise-specific project management education/training and at times standards enforcement (see Figure 6.11).

Enterprise Importance	Key Issue	Activity
Strategic	Personal Mastery	Involve CoP that continually builds master project managers
Tactical	Control	Keep project management consistent and administratively controlled
Operational	Monitoring	Provide generalized education/ training and organization specific acceptable practices.

Project Management Organization
Figure 6.11

Projects of Life – Purchasing as New Home

Identifying the *basics* of a project will make clearer the most appropriate process for achieving its outcome. For purchasing a new home, as for every project, all the *basics* should be considered. However, three highlighted here are *beginning*, *end* and *objective*. If the *beginning* of this project is when the idea first is brought up, perhaps between you and your spouse, then the project will probably be managed with an *evolutionary* approach. The tasks in this project will include attendance at many open houses until there's an agreement on characteristics for the new house (looks, content, neighborhood, etc.). Once these are decided then the *objective* of the project will be formulated around them. The *end* of the project would be when the contract is signed. How long the project takes is relatively arbitrary although it shouldn't go on indefinitely.

As a second case some purchases of new homes are much more driven by their *end* date with well defined *objectives* from the beginning (e.g. four bedrooms within 30 minutes of work). This approach at purchasing a home could be in response to the need for relocating to another city as a result of a new job or promotion where work is to begin immediately. The process of managing the project will be more *monolithic* in nature where events will be planned within firm time constraints.

While purchasing a new home seems like it ought to be managed the same each time, there are circumstances that will shift how one *orients* the tasks of the project – the process used to achieve its outcome. These circumstances can be discovered during an evaluation of the *basics* parameter. One can imagine the confusion that would reign if the two project *objectives* mentioned above (one relatively flexible and the other more well defined) where exchanged for one another. Perhaps you've moved more than a half dozen times in your career and now its time to retire and purchase that "dream home". The *monolithic* process that was used in the past may yield unacceptable results. Like the first case above, the process will probably be much more *evolutionary* as you come to understand what sorts of "dream homes" are out there. Attention to the *basics* of a project can identify an appropriate process to carry it out (such as *evolutionary* or *monolithic*).

Chapter 7

Project Teams

Teamwork is critical to most projects. Great teams are more than a lose collection of individuals supporting social consistency; they are a cohesive group working toward an objective. The project objective may bring a team together so they coalesce in their thinking about what is to be done on the project but there is also a personal commitment to great teamwork. This coalescence when coupled with emotionally-based team cohesion can produce excellent team performance. Coalescence is all about coordination between team members to reach the project's objective – a rational reasonable way to organize the work and communication channels. In contrast the project team cohesiveness is a shared personal attitude between team members. Along with coalescence and cohesion the right kind of team matters for team performance. The kind of team needed will vary by how the team needs to perform to achieve its expected outcome. The need may be for the team to be innovative, to be efficient in an implementation-type project, to be extremely cooperative in a managerial/administrative project, or to be consistent in applying well-known rules in an engineering-type project.

Each kind of team will also need to coalesce and be cohesive to some degree. Team coalescence, cohesion, and kind of team can be associated with the three worlds (see chapter 1) of people, machine, and strategy (see Figure 7.1)

World	Concept(s)
People	Cohesion -Felt community -Personal associations
Machine	Coalescence -Project deliverable -Team organization
Strategy	Kind of team -Enterprise focus -Problem category

The Worlds and Team Concepts
Figure 7.1

NATURE OF TEAMS

The nature of a team can be described by considering its key elements. These elements of a team are the same as one would find when describing organizations, communities, and cultures (Ossorio, 1983). Elements include members, statuses, social practices, decision assumptions, and the language/lingo used. Teams are recognized/identified by their members, teams function where each member has a status, members interact according to their acceptable social practices that take place between both its members and outsiders, members make choices based on accepted decision making assumptions, and communicate with a language or lingo. Being a member of a team implies one special social practice – the one that identifies a person as a member. This accreditation process is a part of team formation (see below). The status each member has can be formally given or informally earned. Project leader is one of particular interest (see chapters 10 and 12). A team's decision-making assumptions can be specifically stated, such as a change approval process, or implied by action such as requiring consensus on an overall design change. Figure 7.2 provides example questions that are associated with the key elements of a team.

Elements of Team	Example Questions
Members	Who are members of the team?
Statuses	Who is the leader?
Social Practices	How does someone become a member?
Decision Assumptions	How are changes handled?
Language/lingo	How should communication take place with outsiders?

Nature of Teams
Figure 7.2

TEAM FORMATION: MEMBERSHIP

Reaching for team perfection is a worthy goal, but may get in the way of getting something done on the project. Members of a team are the keys to understanding the variability in team performance. Various levels of team perfection exist and realizing which level a particular team is on, or aspires to, is a step toward achieving sufficient team cohesion. No matter what the perfect team may be, it usually won't be available when the project begins. Therefore, how perfect should the team be before the project work commences? Three possibilities are worth examing. The first is a nearly perfect team, second an OK team, and third a "who you have available" team. The third may eventually turn out to be a first or second variety, but not because the team was assembled with individual skills and availabilities in mind.

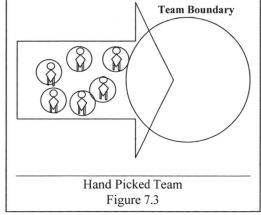

Hand Picked Team
Figure 7.3

Nearly Perfect or Hand Picked

Team members are hand picked from a variety of possibilities and are matched as closely to the work to be performed on the project. A good example of this kind of team is what has been referred to as the "networked" team (Charan, 1991). Project requirements are matched with available people. The project often is of high importance and when competing for resources with other projects this project will come out on top, or close to the top. Projects of this ilk may be critical for survival of the enterprise, or require extreme innovation that the most creative people are "obviously" needed (Katzenbach, J. et. al., 1994) (see Figure 7.3).

Examples of these projects would be those with absolute deadlines (perhaps due to strict regulations), business mergers, first in a set of "roll-outs" where high exposure is expected, or already committed business product deadlines. Also, when a new technology is on trial often a hand picked team is given the job. Subsequent projects using the technology may not have the luxury of having a hand picked team. The false assurance of having proved the technology "works" may lead to less than adequate attention paid to project team coordination. Certain projects may only be successful if a hand picked team is used even if the technology has already proven to be successful. Team formation for the nearly perfect team is best done around the objectives of the project. These teams are usually all about performance, and easily coalesce around the project's objective. The team accreditation process is having been picked in the first place.

When a space launch is planned, the team of astronauts that come together fit the idea of a nearly perfect team. They are motivated toward the objective, usually are willing to go the extra mile to find ways to work together, and are able to maintain focus on the overall goal. Pilots and the crew of most major airlines form nearly perfect teams every time they take to the skies. Most have not worked together before as an entire team, but it doesn't take them long to put all other concerns aside and concentrate on the objective a getting from point "A" to point "B". These teams usually form fast and without the guidance of the project leader.

OK Team

An OK team has a few key members who fit the project's need but also have a number of people who would be second or third choices for the team based on abilities and availability (see Figure 7.4). The key people picked for the project are critical to the team formation. Team formation will require the project leader to provide opportunities for team members to work together and experience an accreditation process. The non-key individuals will experience accreditation once they begin working with the key project group. Key members will have already coalesced around the project and the others will begin becoming part of the team once they "get it". Since the key people are already into the project, materials used and the process of team formation should be project-related rather than extra-project oriented (e.g. an off-site retreat built around games, and/or a group nature experience). The project leader should formulate tasks that can be accomplished fairly quickly and get the key members working with others on these tasks. This will bring the non-key members into a coalescing experience with the key members. It will also accomplish an early "win" that could lead to higher team cohesion.

Who you have Team

Many projects are staffed with who is available. While more risky than the other possibilities, it is the most convenient for organizations to support (see Figure 7.5). Great successes have come out of these kinds of teams when the challenge is clearly communicated. During filming of the *Godfather* Francis Ford Coppola told a young colleague:

Do you still want to direct films? Always remember three things: have a definitive script before you begin to shoot. There'll always be some changes, but they should be small ones. Second, work with people you trust and feel secure with. Remember good crew people you've worked with

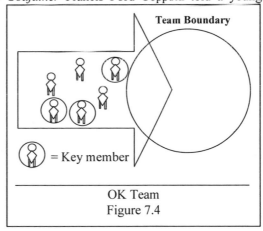

OK Team
Figure 7.4

before and get them for your film. Third, make your actors feel very secure, so they can do their job well. I've managed to do none of these things on this film. (Lebo, 1997)

Clearly Coppola felt his project team was less than the ideal. Yet the Godfather project is one of the most successful of its kind.

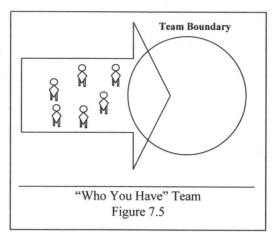

Team Boundary

"Who You Have" Team
Figure 7.5

Team formation for the "who you've have" team will require the project leader use non-project specific team formation activities. In the *Godfather* Coppola, during part of the initial filming, provided dinner on the set around at a large table for the actors and part of the crew. It was not a rehearsal but an actual dinner. The script called for a dinner scene and this team formation activity established behavioral expectations that would effect the real project activity of enacting the film's scene.

Success of a project hinges on people working together, but this togetherness may need to be discovered during the project rather than designed-in up front. John Madden, of football fame, commented on the "family" or togetherness sometimes experience by professional football teams. In his view the togetherness comes from winning and not the other way around. Success begins to establish relationships that may have never taken place between members of a team. Hence, start with "who you have" and look for early "wins". This will contribute to oneness that may save the project in times of chaos.

TEAM COALESENCE

A project team is a group with a purpose. How much that purpose should shape the behavior of the team and the relationship between team members varies with the circumstances of the project. If the project lends itself to careful and detail planning, has a clear direction, is limited by an overall time constraint, and is composed of people who know their jobs and are capable of doing them, then spending a significant amount of time building a team may be wasteful. However, if the project does not lend itself to careful planning, the team members are unclear about what's expected and how they should contribute, then how the project leader deals with team formation may be what propels it along to completion.

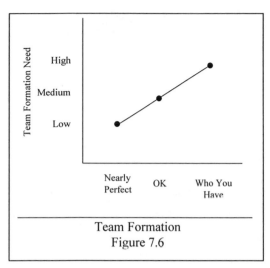

Team Formation
Figure 7.6

One method to coalesce a team around the project's objective is to build it through the steps of *forming, storming, norming, performing,* and *adjourning* (Tuckman, 1977). The *forming* step is when people are unsure of where they are with one another and are unclear about how to share information. *Storming* is when miscommunication is high and many relationships may be strained because they are working out how to say something, and living through confusion. *Norming* is when the reasonable expectations of each person have coalesced in an informal contract. *Performing* is when the team is executing the step to reach the project objective. *Adjourning* is the collection of activities that occurs when the team is disbanded. This approach is based on the team learning how to interact with each other. Learning has been depicted as a four stage process where each stage is identified by the flex-points on the curve. While the learning curve is fundamentally an individual-based phenomenon, it can be applied to groups and organizations as well (Lovinger, 1998; Applegate, 2003). Hence the four stages of learning apply (see Figure 7.7).

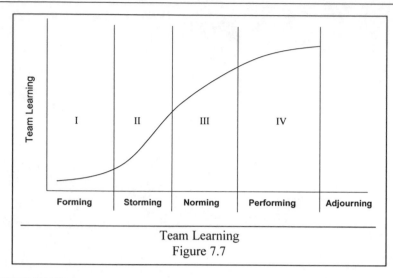

Team Learning
Figure 7.7

TEAM COHENSION

A well functioning team needs a sense of emotional oneness. This sense of cohesion fosters effective communication, as well as producing an end product that is self-consistent.

Three factors are important for developing team cohesion. One is a shared experience. When a group of people share experiences deeply and across a wide expanse of time a culture begins to form. The same phenomenon is true of teams. Before a culture sets in, a group develops a sense of identity that comes from shared experience. This identity is step one in having a cohesive team.

The second factor is to share a primary belief or a fundamental way of picturing the world – a common worldview. The worldview does not need to be a complete set of attitudes or beliefs, but some main element that each member can identify with. It may be a common goal, a common enemy, or even the sense of a common threat. For projects, the project objective may be all that is necessary but don't count on it. Another "higher" or loftier shared belief may be needed. A story circulates about a group of software testers working in IBM. Everyone disliked them, and finding people to participate as members of the testing group was no easy task. Once the group figured out they shared a common belief of protector of quality, they began to act as a cohesive team. They dressed in black and began to achieve a reputation throughout the organization as tough cookies (DeMarco, 1987).

The third factor is a sense of closure. Closure occurs when a task or effort results in a completion – a sense of "doneness". The shared experience of closure provides a sense of group accomplishment and the opportunity to realize "we couldn't have done it without you". This phrase applies to each member of the team, so that what is really shared is a sense of one another's value to the whole. Each time a music rehearsal is concluded, the musicians have the opportunity to feel a sense of closure. Even though the job is not done there is a sense of having completed a step within an overall process. This aspect of projects often gets overlooked – we just go onto the next thing. Many good project managers provide "parties", song-and-dance meetings about what was just completed, a hoopla presentation to a group of stakeholders, etc. The danger in these acts is that they can be easily falsified. If there was no real closure but only its trappings, the team can usually tell, and such instances will erode team culture since it confuses what is really a shared experience. The experience of closure is legitimate and when fictionalized for other gains, team members may become disillusioned (see Figure 7.8).

```
1.  Shared Experience
2.  Shared Belief/Goal
3.  Sense of Closure
_____

Team Cohesion Factors
Figure 7.8
```

How quickly a group experiences cohesion depends on the team's common background, the leader's ability to communicate and provide team building experiences, and the circumstances surrounding the project. In Tom Browkaw's book on *The Greatest Generation* (Brokaw, 1998) we are reminded of the cohesive power of war. Indoctrination into the armed forces, either through boot camp or other training, were team-building experiences. The common enemy was part of the project circumstances and represented a shared belief in what was to be overcome. Closure was experience with every conclusion of an encounter with the enemy. Shared experiences, a common enemy, and experienced closure, created high levels of cohesion that in some instances remained well into the future.

For the OK and "who you've got" teams, if a team can experience these factors before the project officially begins through a team building exercise, work on the project should be more productive right at the outset. Such exercises may go from retreat-like experiences to informal "getting to know you" lunches. Having a team plan and participate in a trip to evaluate software that they may be required to implement is one such opportunity.

Teams have been identified as ineffective through five hierarchical dysfunctions. The first is a lack of trust between members, the second fear of conflict, third a lack of commitment, fourth avoidance of accountability, and fifth inattention to results (Lencioni, 2002). The team may have *coalesced* around the project objectives and even identified the right *kind* of team need (e.g. *innovative*), but these five dysfunctions result from a lack *cohesion* (see Figure 7.9). Trust has to be proven through behaviors that are bound by established relationships; once this begins conflict is acceptable because individuals do not have to be as guarded in their opinions and behaviors. Commitment comes from identity and mutual responsibility from the levels of trust and conflict, and once responsibility between individuals occurs, accountability is not far behind. Results are what the group agrees to be the expected outcome of the effort, and this agreement will focus the group toward measuring themselves by this outcome.

Five Dysfunctions of a Team
Figure 7.9

KINDS OF TEAMS

Temporary and Permanent teams

Over the long run permanent teams are dependent upon the initial team maturation process, but this process is often lost from view of current project participants – it's taken for granted how the team works. These teams need to established good interpersonal relationships at the beginning or they will come back as continuing and nagging problems. There's a lot to be said about getting started off on the right foot. A permanent team has the added burden of providing a new member a way onto the team, an accreditation process. This process could involve performing administrative activities, or even going through a corporate version of hazing. Project leaders, especially from a pure project orientation/style, are responsible for the accreditation process and need to be sensitive to its impact on new and existing project members. As an example, some team members may not be accepted until they have experienced the bad side of being a part of the team. The renowned director John Ford was famous for putting people on the spot. Jimmy Stewart recalled an instance with John Wayne where Wayne essentially accused Stewart of being the "teachers pet" because Stewart had never been put on the spot by Ford in the filming of "The Man Who Shot Liberty Valance". Finally one day Stewart recalls making a comment about a fellow actor's costume. Ford halted production and had everyone come down and reiterated the comment for all to hear, then Ford sent them back to work as if nothing had happened. Stewart felt one inch tall after the incident. Later Wayne approached Stewart and said "Welcome to the club". John Ford had a way of getting the best of his team, and many of them worked together from one film to another (a permanent team that spanned projects).

Cohesive teams know each others strengths and weaknesses, pull together, and compensate for each other to achieve the desired outcome. A cohesive team requires a history of interaction, a shared objective, and a sense of closure (a shared experience of accomplishment). With permanent teams this is much easier to achieve because each project itself is a natural closure point. Temporary teams need to have other closure points built in like milestones or perhaps completing parts of the project over time.

Independent of the permanent/temporary nature of a project team is the structure of the problem they are expected to solve. Some problems are highly structured and require more of a cookie-cutter approach than others. Those with low structure require much more interfacing with outside stakeholders as well as creativity from the project team itself. Figure 7.10 shows four different kinds of teams based on the dimension of team consistency (permanent/temporary), and the clarity of the project's major problem (or objective). A problem with a high structure indicates a well known set of rules for achieving the project outcome One with a low structure indicates relatively unknown rules.

Each project faces a problem to solve whose resolution is usually represented by the primary deliverable of the project. Expectation of team performance will differ depending on the consistency and clarity of the problem as represented by its requirements specificity along with the decision assumptions or rules that are acceptable. Also, the permanence or temporary nature of the team, its lifespan, will play a hand into the expectation of team performance.

Two dimensions of expectations of team performance are the problem's consistency/clarity and the team's lifespan. If the problem and team are consistent/clear the team's major issue is to "get on with it" and *implement* the solution.

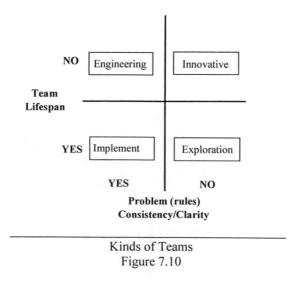

Kinds of Teams
Figure 7.10

Implementation Teams

Clear leadership characterizes these teams. Meetings are usually carried out efficiently, and are focused on solving the problem at hand. Performance is usually measured by clear standards (often financial and time-to-delivery), and work tasks are easily identified and assigned to those with the skills to carry them out.

Hiring a professional crew to install a new driveway for a home owner usually takes on the form of an *implementation* team. There is an expected outcome that is made relatively clear at the beginning, a timeframe given to perform the project, and a clear financial commitment made. The professional crew has performed similar installs many times, and once agreement is reached with the owner they simply get on with it (not that things can't and haven't gone wrong in the past with these sorts of projects, but they are usually clear and well understood).

Engineering Teams

These teams function on a professional level based on knowledge. Rules are usually well defined and the major issue is to find a way to share the expertise of the team's members. A great deal of time is often spent on structuring the problem of the project, then solving it efficiently with a high degree of reliability of the solution. Good and best practices are sought and individual team members are expected to know these and interact accordingly. When necessary, new solution processes or tools may be created to "get at" the problem and its solution.

Building a new rollercoaster ride at an amusement park requires an *engineering* team. The mechanics and structural necessities are relatively clear, but how they are arranged together to produce the desired ride is something that must be worked out between those with the relevant knowledge. As a way of structuring the problem a model of the rollercoaster may be used to assess areas of difficulties.

Innovative Teams

Often these teams experience shared leadership where the leadership role shifts from time to time. The specific purpose or objective of the project is its constant guiding light, and is used by the leader as the way to orient the work. Individual tasks to meet the goal may be impossible to plan, and if made too specific, may obscure the objective since the process to reach it is emergent, ambiguous, and equifinal (multiple outcomes could solve the same problem) (Weick, 1979). Innovative teams spend a great deal of time finding the real problem, not constructing its solution. Meetings are often very open-ended and may conclude with various opinions about what happened, if anything.

An electrical power company used an *innovative* team to design a new safety program to keep their linemen from falling. They met together as expert linemen and worked through a variety of solution possibilities before formulating a new program and specific tools and processes for climbing safety. At the beginning of the project there was lots of ambiguity since they had no idea what the new safety program should be, but their goal of reduced linemen accidents and deaths was clear.

Exploration Teams

These teams construct coalitions of people who identify with one another and can bring their talents to any problem that may present itself. Team members may continually challenge assumptions, but the integrity of any member is seldom challenged. Usually these teams face many problems at once, and their strength is to be able to prioritize or filter them (Perkins, 2000).

Acquiring another business is a complicated project and an *exploration* team may be used. They will need to form coalitions within the organization to make sure the outcome of the merger does not seriously impact the current business in a negative way. A history of working together in the past, a characteristic of an *exploration* team, brings trust to the process, and allows the team to execute the acquisition even though issues will continually arise that could not be planned for.

See Figure 7.11 for a comparison across teams considering several team characteristics.

	Kinds of Teams			
Team Characteristics	**Construction**	**Engineering**	**Innovative**	**Exploration**
Problem Strength	Solving	Structuring	Finding	Filtering
Team role assumptions	Coordination	Professional	None	Coalition
Leadership challenge	Delegation	Specialties	Changes	Mission Clarity
Meetings	Clear/Efficient	Clear/Wandering	Unclear/Inefficient	Unclear/Quick

Characteristics of Kinds of Teams
Figure 7.11

TEAM ORGANIZATION

Teams are a collection of possible relationships between project leaders, project members, and project stakeholders. With these three roles, various team organizational structures are possible. These include leader-centric teams; domain knowledge teams (stakeholder dominant); technology specialty teams; and equality teams. The dominant role for each of these teams is different. In the leader-centric team the project leader role is dominant, in the domain knowledge team the key outside stakeholder is dominant, in the specialty team the project member role is dominant, and in the equality team there is no dominant role (see Figure 7.12).

Role Dominance	Team Name
Leader	Chief team
Stakeholder	Domain team
Member	Specialty team
None	Equality team

Role Dominance and Team Name
Figure 7.12

Leader-Centric (Chief team)

The leader of the team is its primary working chief. All others are there to support this chief in developing the project deliverables (see Figure 7.13). The leader is one of great talent with a strong drive to complete the work. Such leaders may even be classified a "workaholics" because they are constantly at work, chewing on and solving every technical problem or domain knowledge requirement presented to them. These leaders have been referred to as chief surgeons (Mills, 1983). Other team members are charged with providing support services when needed to the chief. There is evidence that some people possess that quality to out-perform the normal technology professional by several magnitudes. With one person doing the actual work there remains a strong likelihood the results will be highly consistent and self-integrating.

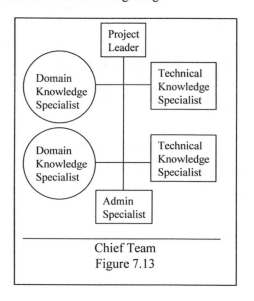

Chief Team
Figure 7.13

An example of a chief team is a ramrod putting up the "big top" for a three-ring circus. The ramrod gets it done with grips, individual performers, electrical, and mechanical specialists. You get the feeling the ramrod could do it alone if time permitted. One instance of this at a university is where a lone developer designed and built a student information system for the entire campus of thousands of students. Help was given at the behest of the chief developer, but he did all the detail work. Later in his career, after being promoted to a high leadership role in the finance arm of the central administration, he developed the entire structure by which schools and other major entities of the university shared overhead costs. This required extreme energy, coordination between divergent groups, and high creativity. He had help, but was its chief architect and developer. Implementation of sophisticated off-the-shelf software applications or tools usually requires the assistance of a highly skilled consultant. In some instances the consultant acts as the chief surgeon for the entire project.

Domain Knowledge Team

Project teams can be organized by the knowledge domains of the project's objective. For IT projects knowledge domains are usually represented by different user communities or stakeholders. One community may have little or no knowledge of the others' area. IT specialists are assigned to each domain (see Figure 7.14). The most important aspect of projects utilizing this team approach is what the result is expected to do, the need for domain knowledge within the project overwhelms other aspects such as technical specialty knowledge. A factory layout project is a good example where what is to be performed by the factory is more important than how it is constructed. For information technology projects the technology piece may be considered more or less standard, but what the system actually does and how it does it is tantamount. The project is broken down into key elements according to the knowledge domains. There may be a set of domain experts responsible for these elements, or in the case of IT, the primary user may actually be appointed to the project leadership role.

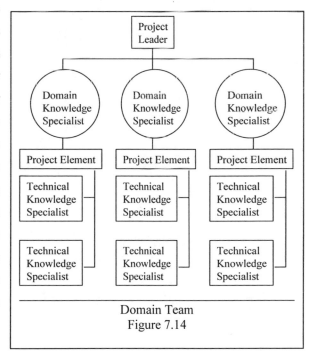

Domain Team
Figure 7.14

Technology Specialty Team

The key aspect of this team structure is technical skill specialization (see Figure 7.15). In the case of IT the technical specialists are pooled, and work on every segment of the project. Domain knowledge is of secondary importance for the project's success.

Domain knowledge may be trivial or already understood by the stakeholders. The project is not so much about discovery of domain knowledge and its automation, but about the automation aspect itself. Each project element may require several specialties.

A construction team would be an example of this team style with electricians, plumbers, and carpenters, etc. each working on every floor of a multi-story building. For IT projects IT professionals provide their expertise within each subsystem of a large integrated system. Managing the specialties is the key aspect of this type of team structure.

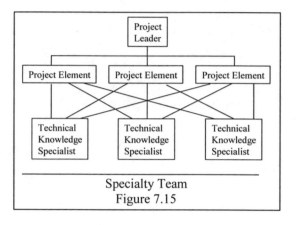

Specialty Team
Figure 7.15

Equality Team

The *equality* team, or egoless team is where each team member is considered interchangeable with the others (see Figure 7.16). Leadership of such a team may even change as circumstances require, but within the team. Specialties within domain areas and even technology areas are blurred. Knowledge of the domain and specialties are equally shared where no one is expected to have appreciably more talent in any area than another. Egoless teams were identified a number of years ago in the IT area (Weinberg, 1971) where each team member is an equal critic of others and examine one another's work – called walk-thrus. One positive aspect of *equality* teams is sharing knowledge as the project unfolds. Since everyone working on the project functions in an equal way, the outcome will usually look and fell consistent. For IT projects this may be a very important outcome especially when the system is somewhat complex and is expected to be easy to learn. Learning to use one part of the system would be consistent with learning another part.

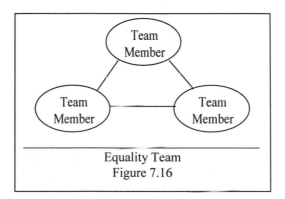

Equality Team
Figure 7.16

There are so many possible team aspects a few are combined here to get a feel for the possibilities. In a reasonably perfect world they would match up into four possibilities (see Figure 7.17). How one manages a project has a great deal to do with assessing the team specifics and then taking action to achieve the desired outcome of the project. The suggestion here is to find the kind of problem, form the kind of team needed to solve it, and structure the team in the most optimal way.

Project Problem	Kinds of Teams	Team Structure
Solving	Construction	Domain Knowledge
Structuring	Engineering	Specialty
Finding	Innovative	Equality
Filtering	Exploration	Leader-centric

Aspects of Teams Matched in a Perfect World
Figure 7.17

PART FOUR

Techniques

Many projects require the usage of techniques for planning and managing detail tasks. Techniques could be anything from planning at a detail level, through establishing a Work Breakdown Structure (WBS), to controlling techniques by monitoring each activity on the project and reporting variance against the plan.

Reporting on these techniques is done with standard reports such as the Gantt chart, cumulative cost curve, and the resource histogram. The intelligence needed to create these detail reports requires planning the relationships between activities, estimating durations, and assigning resources to each activity.

The network of project activities needs to be understood by the project manager in order to make intelligent decision about priorities for resources and cost. Software is usually used to perform network calculations but in most cases a network, once established, will have to be debugged. Debugging a network requires a deep understanding not provided by simply using software. This debugging effort initiates a new understanding and insight on how to manage the project. The project manager begins to master the project itself.

Chapter 8

Planning Techniques

Planning is happening all around us, and its especially critical if the planned objective is to be met through a project management approach. Many people plan before they go to the grocery store, good sports teams have a game plan, serious holiday shoppers often have a plan (usually a list with possible locations to find the items), many ardent vacationers plan their time away, and even excellent teachers may be found working on their lesson plans.

The main point of project formal planning techniques is to transform an abstract idea into a tangible document. The document can be used for agreeing on the overall objective of the project, for deciding who needs to do what and when, and/or for assessing the value of taking the next steps to formalize a project. Four steps to produce a detailed plan document are: Step one, developing an informal task list; step two, formulating a work breakdown structure (WBS) that includes formulating task descriptors; step three, producing a schedule of activities; and step four, assigning resources/people to the schedule. While there are many other parts of project planning, these schedule-oriented pieces are critical for achieving a high level of project planning.

Step One: Developing a Task List

A project may be too big to internalize all at once, so it should be divided into elements of work. Three major approaches can be used to bring out these elements of work. One is a bottom-up approach through brainstorming, another a top-down approach through progressive decomposition into a final operational level of tasks, and the third a mixture of the other two where some of the project is identified through a top-down and another through a bottom-up approach (see Figure 8.1).

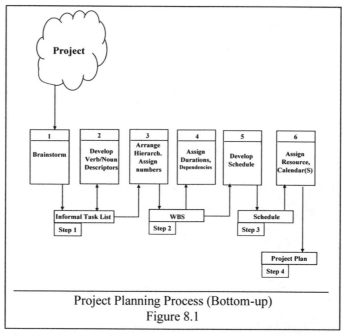

Project Planning Process (Bottom-up)
Figure 8.1

Brainstorming is a popular approach for producing details of a larger domain. It requires people to interact in ways that lifts the problem from obscurity to awareness at a level of detail that makes it understandable and actionable. If your project is to build a four-lane bridge across a railway, then identifying the tasks that need to be accomplished can be done by people identifying everything that comes to mind relevant to this project. Even people not familiar with construction projects are able to devise a decent list of tasks. The brainstorming process frees the knowledge within a group of participants. Rules of brainstorming are:

1. There are no bad ideas
2. Criticism of ideas in not permitted
3. Every idea needs to be recorded briefly (preferable so others can see them)
4. Hitchhiking on others' ideas is encouraged
5. It takes encouraging by a coordinator (people will give up too soon or not
   participate)

The top down approach is accomplished by focusing attention on the high-level functions or items to be performed. In the bridge example, the coordinator may ask: "What are the four or five major items that must be accomplished?" Once these are determined, then they are each broken out into more detail. This continues until the tasks are at a level to be actionable. While the list has some organization about it, it still needs to be cleaned up.

Step Two: Developing the Work Breakdown Structure

After developing a task list through brainstorming or functional decomposition the list needs to be cleaned up. Remove the duplicates, identify similar items and make sure they're different, put similar tasks together, examine tasks for their legitimacy for this project and throw out those that don't make sense or may not actually be part of the project. From the cleansed list, group similar tasks together under a group item. Also, make sure each task has a verb/noun combination such as "paint lines", "draw blueprint", etc. Without the verb the statement is not something that requires action – e.g. "beautiful bridge", "wide blueprint". What's needed is "build beautiful bridge", "draw wide blueprint". Later you may embellish these tasks descriptors with descriptions that identify more specifics. With the tasks descriptors developed, and having them ordered in a hierarchical structure results in a Work Breakdown Structure (WBS). Each task listed in the WBS should also be numbered using a logical numbering scheme. One such scheme is to use decimals for tasks below group tasks – e.g. 2.2.1, 2.2.2, 2.2.3 all belong to group task item 2.2 (see Figure 8.2).

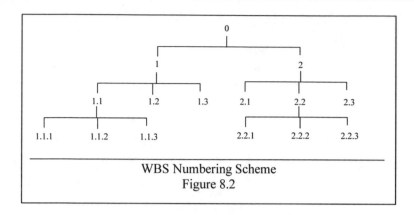

WBS Numbering Scheme
Figure 8.2

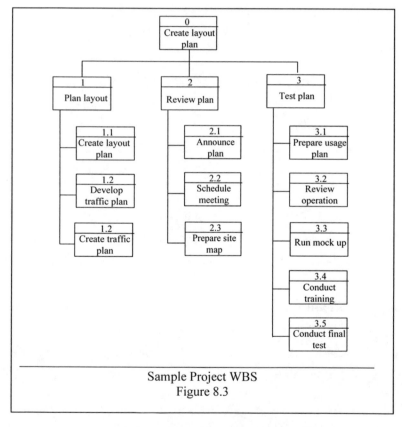

Sample Project WBS
Figure 8.3

Suppose a task list was produced for updating a factory layout. From the task list we have hierarchically arrange the tasks into a WBS and provide IDs and numbers (see Figure 8.3)

While it appears the WBS represents precedent relationships it does not. It does not show the order in which activities should be performed. The WBS provides a way to conceptualize the project, but has little to do with which activity should be performed before/after others. Precedent relationships have to be explicitly assigned for each task. Relationships are assigned in the next step in project planning.

Step Three: Producing A Schedule

Precedent relationships and durations of each task need to be established. Assigning precedent relationships and estimating durations for each task will produce a network of tasks where calculations for the start and finish of each task can be made. Tasks, once in network form, are often referred to as activities. Activities are usually organized into an activity report showing their WBS number, ID, descriptors, precedent relationships, and durations (see Figure 8.4).

WBS	ID	Activity Descriptor	Duration	Immediate Predecessors
1.1	A	Predict sales	3	-
1.2	B	Investigate competitive pricing	4	-
1.3	C	Price sales	3	A,B
2.1	D	Prepare production schedules	2	A
2.2	E	Cost production	5	D
2.3	F	Prepare budget	2	C,E

Activity Report
Figure 8.4

From the activity report a network can be drawn that portrays the relationships between activities, and if done carefully, can be used to show the results of calculations for each activity's start and finish dates. Figure 8.5 shows how one could layout the activity information from Figure 8.4 where the activity is on the arrow – the Arrow Diagramming Method (ADM). Figure 8.6 shows the same network with the activity in the node. This is called the Precedence Diagramming method (PDM). In the ADM the activity is on the arrow while in the PDM the activity is in the node. Figure 8.7 is a network with more activities for a project to design and build a new product in an ADM format. Figure 8.8 shows activity information in a PDM format. Numbers on the arrows connecting the nodes are delays (lags) between the activities (e.g. there is a 4 day delay between *Hire General Manager* and *Order Materials*).

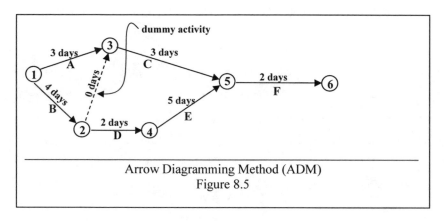

Arrow Diagramming Method (ADM)
Figure 8.5

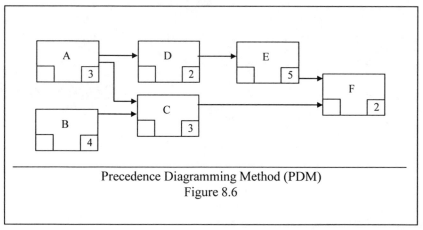

Precedence Diagramming Method (PDM)
Figure 8.6

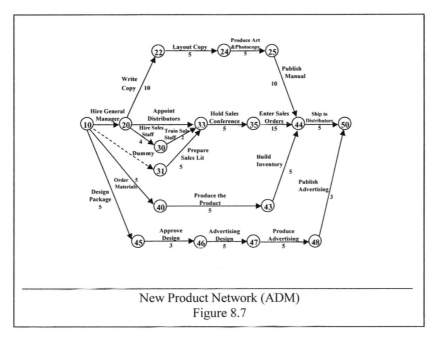

New Product Network (ADM)
Figure 8.7

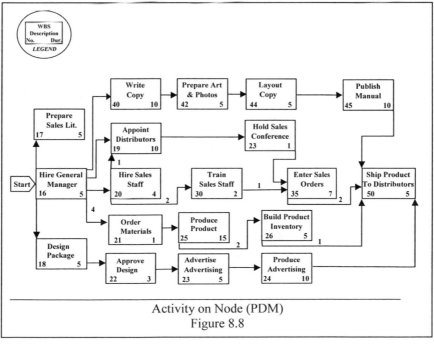

Activity on Node (PDM)
Figure 8.8

When drawing a network with the ADM a dummy activity may be required to maintain network logic and have each activity have a unique set of node numbers. If two activities have the same node numbers, they are really not different activities (see Figure 8.9).

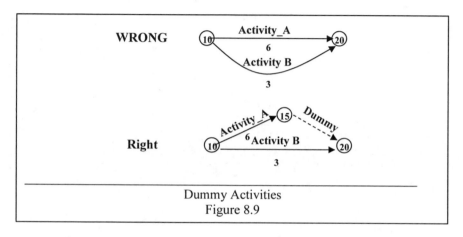

Dummy Activities
Figure 8.9

An algorithm for drawing a network is provided in Figure 8.9.

1. Draw a START node
2. Draw an arrow emanating from the start node to each unconstrained activity (i.e. those with no predecessors)
3. Label the arrows with activity names or identifiers.
4. Scan the list of undrawn activities, for those which have all of their predecessors already drawn:
  - Bring all its predecessors together into a single node.
  - Draw the activity to emanate from that node
5. If two activities have the same beginning and end node, a dummy is needed
  - It should be inserted from the end of one of them to the end of the other
6. If two activities share some, but not all predecessors, a dummy is needed
  - Draw from the node at which the common predecessors end to the node at which the unique predecessors end.
7. Iterate steps 4 - 6 until all activities have been drawn.
8. Bring together to a common END node all activities having no

Algorithm for Drawing a Network (ADM)
Figure 8.10

There are two useful calculated sets of dates for each activity on a network. How soon each activity can start or finish so the project can be completed as soon as possible, and how late each activity can start and finish without impacting the earliest the project can possible be over (how long can an activity be delayed to start/end without impacting the earliest possible start of all its successors). The early dates are computed on a forward pass through the network, and the late dates on a backward pass.

On the forward pass each activity's start date is computed as the earliest the activity can possibly start. Its finish date will be how early it can finish. The early finish (EF) of an activity is it's early start (ES) plus its duration (DUR).

$$EF = ES + DUR$$

The ES of each activity is the latest EF of all its predecessors. The reason for this is that an activity cannot start until all its predecessors are completed. Figure 8.11 shows how this is done. Numbers are used instead of dates at this point for simplicity. Each of the numbers can be converted into a real date by applying a work calendar where each date represents a work time unit on the project (e.g. 14 may represent February 3 if February 3 is the 14th work day of the project).

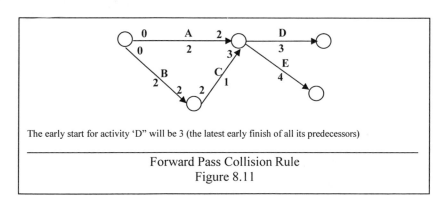

The early start for activity 'D" will be 3 (the latest early finish of all its predecessors)

Forward Pass Collision Rule
Figure 8.11

Once the forward pass is accomplished, the late dates can be computed on a backward pass through the network. Here we are interested in how late an activity can finish without impacting its successors. Begin with the last activity in the network and use its early finish as the late finish and compute it's late start. The late start (LS) of an activity is it's late finish (LF) minus its duration.

$$LS = LF - DUR$$

The LF of an activity is the earliest late start of all its successors. An activity cannot finish any later than the earliest start all those that come after it. (see Figure 8.12).

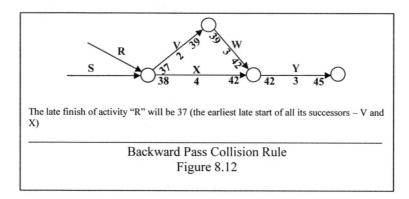

The late finish of activity "R" will be 37 (the earliest late start of all its successors – V and X)

Backward Pass Collision Rule
Figure 8.12

When an activity has its early dates different than its late dates it has float. The activity does not have to start on the ES date, it can float until its late start. Float for each activity is:

$$Float = LS - ES \quad or \quad Float = LF - EF$$

Activities with no float are on the critical path. Critical path activities are those that, if delayed, will delay the end of the project.

Figure 8.13 shows an activity report for the factory layout project shown in the previous WBS (Figure 8.3). The network (ADM) with its calculated early and late dates is shown in Figure 8.14. Notice, the critical path is shown by the heavy lines.

WBS	ID	Activity Descriptor	Duration	Immediate Predecessors
1.1	A	Create factory layout plan	3	-
1.2	B	Develop factory usage plan	4	-
1.3	C	Develop traffic plan	3	-
2.1	D	Announce plan	2	A
2.2	E	Schedule meetings	5	A
2.3	G	Prepare site map	2	B
3.1	H	Prepare ops usage training	6	B
3.2	I	Review operation	4	D,E
3.3	J	Run mock traffic	10	C
3.4	K	Conduct training	3	H,J
3.5	L	Final operational test	4	G,I,K

Factory Update Plan Sample – Activity Report
Figure 8.13

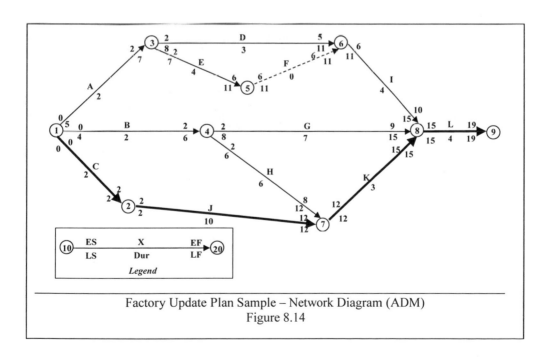

Factory Update Plan Sample – Network Diagram (ADM)
Figure 8.14

A work calendar for the project is needed in order to translate the numeric values into dates. Most people are not scheduled to work on the weekend, so if an activity has duration of 4 and is scheduled to start on Friday, it will not be done until Wednesday evening the following week (or Thursday morning). A work calendar is produced by explicitly deciding which dates are workdays and which are not, plus assigning the beginning date of the project (see Figure 8.15).

Sun	Mon	Tue	Wed	Thur	Fri	Sat
Feb 1 --	Feb 2 13	Feb 3 14	Feb 4 15	Feb 5 16	Feb 6 17 ▬▬ 1	Feb 7 --
Feb 8 --	Feb 9 18 ▬▬ 2	Feb 10 19 3	Feb 11 20 4	Feb 12 21	Feb 13 22	Feb 14 --

Work Calendar
Figure 8.15

Step Four: Producing the Detailed Plan (Assigning Resources)

Assigning resources (people) to activities should be as a separate step from developing the initial schedule from calculating early and late dates for the activities. They represent one more constraint on the project besides activity durations and relationships. NEVER assign resources until after the initial set of calculations are completed (early and late dates). After the initial schedule is computed the project manager can see which activities are on the critical path (those with zero float) and how much float the non-critical activities have. Resource assignments can be made much more intelligently if the float on each activity is known. Those on the critical path should be given priority consideration when assigning resources.

Each resource (person or skill type) may have it's own work calendar. This is one more complication for the project manager to deal with, but if a high level of detail planning with resources is needed, then the project will require multiple work calendars.

After resources are assigned to activities a new set of early and late dates will need to be calculated given the additional resource constraints. If the dates are the same, then there are either unlimited resources, a mistake has been made, or luck has raised its beautiful head. Most of the time the additional constraint of resources on a project will push the end date of the project out into the future.

Project Plan Graphical Reports

The project schedule can be shown using a Gantt chart (also referred to as a bar chart). At he top of Figure 8.17 the beginning of each activity is show by an "up" triangle, and the finish with a "down" triangle. A line spanning the time units between the "up" and "down" triangles represents the duration of an activity.

A resource histogram is shown in the middle of Figure 8.17. It shows the planned usage of people across time in a step-type chart. The histogram shows how many people will be required to work on the project for each time frame. Since it takes some time for a project to "ramp up" fewer resources are usually required at the beginning. Also, fewer are usually required at the end because at this point in the project things are winding down and can be completed with fewer people.

Cost on a project is usually reported graphically with an "S-cost" curve (see bottom of Figure 8.17). This curve shows accumulated cost of a project over time. Just like resource usage, the cost starts off smaller, advances considerably during the project, and falls off on the end.

Danger of Over-Planning

Planning from the ground up, as with the brainstorming approach, may produce a very logical outcome that makes complete sense but does not capture the real complexity of the project. The plan does not include possible changes that will inevitably come, nor accommodate measurement inaccuracies of the estimated durations for each task.

Program Evaluation Review Techniques (PERT) is one way to deal with inaccuracies of estimates by requiring three estimates for each task (an optimal, a pessimistic, and a most likely). By using deviations, probability statements can be made about when a task, or the entire project, will be completed (Mills, 1962). Monte Carlo and the critical chain methods are also effective ways to deal with planning uncertainty.

Even with PERT, accounting for changes, or assuming all the activities of a project have been identified is still uncertain. Research has shown that when there are missing branches in a tree of understanding, people will over-attribute what they think they know about the branches that are present and consequently under-attribute what they don't know (they think they know more than they really do). When the knowledge remains the same but the branches representing that knowledge decreases, people will increase their tendency to over-attribute what they know (Browdy, 2007).

For anticipated positive results people also value certainty of outcomes higher than for outcomes merely probable. Certainty in the positively framed results is more attractive (I'd rather have 4 sure breaks a day than a 50% chance to have eight). This is referred to as the pseudo-certainty effect (Tversky, 1981).

Plans are more likely to get approved if they appear certain that if they appear uncertain. Uncertainty is often expressed by a probability of success (an argument **against** using PERT for project approval) rather than as a certainty with a modicum of expected surprises. The more detail in the plan the more certain it appears. The best planning strategy is to make sure all the branches of the plan (WBS) are present but not go too deep when the details are uncertain (see Figure 8.16). Planning a project in too much detail may work against facing reality and preparing for uncertain events.

Planning and plans are needed for most projects, but hiding risk within the mask of detailed positive-spun plans is dangerous. Our tendency as humans is to over-specify when we actually don't know details. This tendency can be ameliorated by explicitly identifying risks.

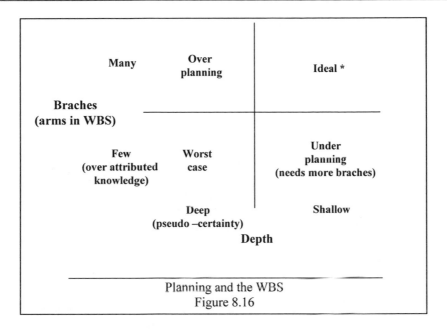

Planning and the WBS
Figure 8.16

Project planners will tend to present project plans with more certainty than they should. Individuals over attribute their control of situations especially if the outcome is positive. These issues coupled with the common practice to be optimistic will result in plans that may not be close to reality. This *insider view* produces a project plan as if one had perfect insider knowledge about what will occur. An *outsider view* finds a project outside of the current one, and makes comparisons against it – a reality check (Lovallo, 2003). The *outsider view*, of planning involves:

1. Selecting a reference class of projects

2. Assessing the distribution of outcomes (in numeric form – how long/much)

3. Making an intuitive prediction of your project's position in the distribution

4. Assessing the reliability of your prediction

5. Correcting the intuitive estimate

By using the *outsider view* projects can be baselined quickly and then adjusted for specifics. This is taking advantage of the *anchoring/adjustment* heuristic (Tversky, 1974). With this heuristic people over-attribute the accuracy of their original estimate, thus making adjustments from *it* rather than starting in a new place (even when the situation warrants starting over). Hence, the starting reference project will set the stage for more realistic planning. An outsider view gives a better starting reference point than the overly-optimistic insider view.

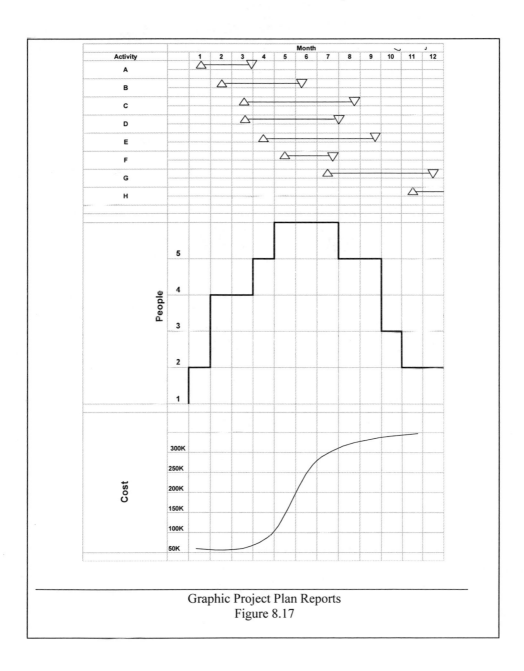

Graphic Project Plan Reports
Figure 8.17

Chapter 9

Control Techniques

Introduction

Project managers use various control techniques to keep projects on track. Some projects require more control than others, and some by their nature are almost uncontrollable such as those using novel technology or whose outcome is unclear. Yet even near uncontrollable projects need to be subjected to a controlling process for reporting and mid-stream correction. Various levels of control are possible. A high level of control can be instituted by closely monitoring the activities and milestones so that early warning of being off track is evident. A medium level of control includes moderate reporting on individual activities coupled with ensuring milestones completions are viewed as critical targets. A low level of control is represented by little attention to individual activities, and moderate attention to milestone completions. Control includes elements of schedule control, cost control, and resource control. Resource control usually is concerned with people as the resource, but could include other kinds of resources such as cost, equipment and space (see Figure 9.1).

	CONTROL		
Monitoring Source	**Low**	**Med**	**High**
Project Activities	Little	Some	Much
Planned Milestone	Some	Much	Much

Degree of Control
Figure 9.1

Schedule control

Monitoring a project schedule is critical if the timing of events and conclusion of the project are at the top of stakeholders' agendas. The importance of timing, or completions, may be important for every activity on the project, every milestone, as well as the end date. On some projects the only timing issue is the end date itself, and on others timing is subservient to cost or resource usage. If timing of both activities and end date are critical, weekly variance reports showing how each activity is progressing according to plan should be used and discussed with key stakeholders and published to all concerned parties. One cannot monitor a project any more closely than it is planned, so if high control is needed then a high level of planning will be required. This could include detail activity planning using Critical Path Method (CPM), Program Evaluation Review Technique (PERT), and other such planning/control disciplines.

"Actual" data need to be collected and applied against the plan to arrive at a variance -- the difference between plan versus actual. A rule of thumb for an acceptable level of variance for highly controlled projects is dependent upon the approach used to plan the project. If PERT was used then probability of expected completion dates for the project can be computed. These are a function of the variance on each activity on the expected critical path. Estimating activities with maximum allowable estimates on the low side provides a high level of control. Each activity should be estimated no longer than the duration between control meetings. For example, if project control review meetings are a week apart, then each activity should be estimated no longer than 5 days.

This means that every activity on the project should be completed inside of two control points. The control points may be referred to as milestones or simply as project review. Also, by using longer activity estimated durations less schedule control will result (see Figure 9.2).

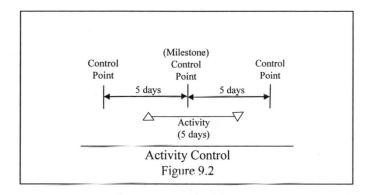

Activity Control
Figure 9.2

More milestones or control points will increase the level of control. A milestone is a significant project event which is usually used as a control point (e.g. the completion of formal planning). A control point could be the completion of a phase where a deliverable is provided, or an artificial "made-up" date or cyclical event (e.g. monthly milestone meeting to review progress). For projects with a high level of control, there will be less acceptable variance, relatively more control points and milestones, and an estimating rule-of-thumb that is smaller than normal.

Cost Control

Once a project is approved it usually falls within a cost constraint based on that approval. Many technology-orientated projects are done based on Cost-Benefit Analysis (CBA), and for others cost may be based on very loose guidelines. If cost is a way to measure success, strategic projects may not be attempted. If *experimental* projects are important to stay abreast of competition, then cost control needs to be very flexible. If the project's intention is to change the way people think about how they work (*cultural intention*), then cost control will require flexibility due to the unfolding and unforeseen impact. Overall guidelines for cost control as they relate to project intentions are depicted in Figure 9.3. The overall intention of a project should inform the project manager on how much control is needed.

Intentions	Cost Control
Experimental	Very little & Flexible
Process Change	Heavy (CBA, ROI, EVA)
Strategic Change	Moderate (EVA)
Cultural Change	Some & Flexible

Intentions and Cost Control
Figure 9.3

There are various cost approaches available to project managers. For projects requiring a high level of cost control a CBA or an Earned Value Analysis (EVA) approach may be used. These two approaches are ways to account for financial investments in a project across time. If the project is to be completed in less than two years, then these approaches may be too formal and distractive. More informal methods if monitoring costs should be used. These more formal approaches rely on ideas such as:

Return on Investment (ROI)
Present Value (PV)
Net Present Value Discounted Cash Flow (NPV)
Internal Rate of Return (IRR)
Earned Value Analysis (EVA)

ROI is a calculation widely used for projects that involve considerable asset investment along with expectations for operational improvements in the business. Making equipment maintenance more efficient provides an example. An investment in an information system development project to improve maintenance can be weighed against gains realized in maintenance activities. While operating income can be used to compute expected income from a new investment, in the maintenance systems case it is operating efficiencies as measured by reduced operating costs. Assume with the maintenance system we could save $100,000 per year, so in the ROI approach:

Rate of Return on Investment = Operating Income/Invested Assets

For five years: ROI = $1,500,000/project cost

The project cost would include people, equipment, administrative, and other costs associated with the project. Following is an example reviewed in a rough form, then using a more formal accounting approach.

Assume the cost of capital is 8%. If money is borrowed now to invest in a project ($250,000), that money will cost 8% a year. If the project takes four years, then the cost is computed by the compound interest formula:

$$(1 + Rate)^{Years} \times Amount$$

$$(1 + .08)^4 \times 250,000 = 340,122$$

Most operational efficiency projects are argued on a cost savings basis. So if savings is $100,000 (or so) a year after the project is completed, and it will require a one time investment of $250,000, then in the four years the NPV of the 2$250,000 will be about $350,000 (rounding up from $340,122 – see above). This means it will take us approximately an additional 3 ½ years to recover our investment (this is $100,000 savings per year expected once the project is complete).

In the formal approach you need to look at the realized savings due to usage of the maintenance system after its four years of development, the present value of that savings, and the accumulated, or net present value of the savings (savings will not really be $100,000 per year but what this money would be worth in those future years). As it turns out using NPV to compute the recovery our initial cost of $250,000 will be almost nine years. If we compare this to a project that will take one year to develop for $250,000, its payback will be less than five years (a more realistic hurdle) (see Figure 9.4 and 9.5).

Period	Investment	Savings	PV	NPV
1	250,000	0		(250,000)
2		0		(250,000)
3		0		(250,000)
4		0		(250,000)
5		100,000	66,700	(183,300)
6		100,000	62,900	(120,400)
7		100,000	58,500	(61,900)
8		100,000	54,100	(7,800)
9		100,000	50,000	42,200

NPV for The Four-Year Development Project Example
Figure 9.4

Maintenance Project				
Period	Investment	Savings	PV	NPV
1	250,000	0		(250,000)
2		100,000	85,500	(164,500)
3		100,000	79,400	(85,100)
4		100,000	73,500	(11,600)
5		100,000	66,700	55,100

NPV for the One-Year Development Project Example
Figure 9.5

Usually NPV is used in financial problems to compute return on investment, where the return is based on actual income rather than cost avoidance. If the reason our maintenance system was developed was to sell it to others, then the traditional ROI would account for income generated over time to offset the investment (see Figure 9.6) – not a cost avoidance approach but an income generating one. Looking at an investment of $250,000 for 5 years with cost of capital at 8%:

NPV = Present value of cash inflows – Investment
FV = Future Value

$PV = FV/(1 + Rate)^{Years}$

For period 4 (as an example):
$PV = 60,000/(1+.08)^5 = 40,000$

Maintenance Project				
Period	Expense	Cash Inflows	Net Profit	PV
1	0	0	0	0
2	40,000	20,000	(20,000)	(13,333)
3	30,000	110,000	80,000	53,333
4	20,000	170,000	150,000	100,000
5	20,000	260,000	240,000	160,000
NPV				300,000

NPV For Investment/Profit Example
Figure 9.6

Results show that our initial investment of $250,000 in 3 years will yield a profit of over $50,000 (in today's money).

This all begs the strategic question, do I use innovation to reduce costs or to generate income. In reality is both, and then the questions is how to balance these usages. Projects with cost avoidance approaches are usually easier to justify if there is a good cost accounting structure in place. Income or revenue projections are usually looked upon with some skepticism since they involve unknown future possibilities rather than present realities. However, without strategic innovations some enterprise may find themselves losing business to competitors with customers substituting your business product/service for new or different solutions.

CBA/ROI are useful tools for large projects that have expected measurable payback. These sorts of techniques are especially important for obtaining project approvals in high-control type organizations. EVA is a technique that can be used to monitor the added value during work on the project.

Cost reports are usually shown as cumulative costs over the time of the project (see Figure 9.7). They are often referred to as "S" cost curves.

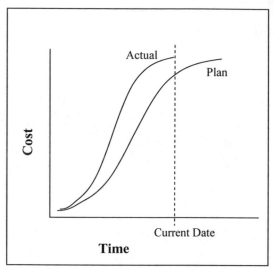

Cumulative "S" Cost Curve
Figure 9.7

Other cost calculations may become important if the project requires adherence to reporting standards. To report on Budgeted Cost of Work Performed (BCWP), costs have to be monitored for each activity in the project. These activities are usually connected to a formal schedule tying back to a Work Breakdown Structure (WBS) that identifies a particular requirement. The Actual Cost of Work Performed (ACWP) may be different than the budgeted, and some projects will require these both be reported (see Figure 9.8).

Maintenance Project				
Activity	Activity Cost (budgeted)	Percent Complete	BCWP	ACWP
A	2,500	100	2,500	3,200
B	4,000	50	2,000	2,200
C	3,000	0	0	0
Total			4,500	5,400

Budgeted Cost of Work Performed (BCWP)
Figure 9.8

Another term, Budget Cost of Work Scheduled (BCWS), is used where the percent complete of an activity in the schedule is used to compute the scheduled cost of that activity. The difference between BCWP and BCWS is that BCWP relies of percent of cost expended, while BCWS relies on planned work activities actual completions (see Figure 9.9).

How the information is gathered for "actuals" is critical for project control. The information can come from a formal time-reporting system (which is often the case), a separate reporting system set up for the project, or interviews with those performing the work (either formally or causally).

Measure	Name	
ROI	Return On Investment	Ratio of money gained or lost on an investment relative to the amount of money invested
CBA	Cost Benefit Analysis	Total expected costs against the total expected benefits of a project in order to decide its viability
BCWP	Budgeted Cost of Work Performed	Budgeted cost of work that has been performed in a scheduled of tasks during a specific time period
BCWS	Budgeted Cost of Work Scheduled	The planned cost amount of the tasks budgeted to be completed during a specific time period
ACWP	Actual Cost of Work Performed	Actual cost that has been used for tasks completed in a time period
EVA	Earned Value Analysis	Used BCWP called Earned Value (EV), BCWS called Planned Value (PV), and compares them against ACWP (or Actual Cost - AC).

Project Planning and Control Measures
Figure 9.9

Resource control

The critical resources for most technical projects are the people. Planning for their usage and then acquiring them when needed is a fundamental project management skill.

If the effort is a *pure project* then the resources are under the project manager's control and assigning them work, etc. is made simpler than if they actually worked in a *functional specialty* department and work on multiple projects at once.

The most common errors in balancing resource need is to assume each person can be as productive as every other person, and the work is so flexible that adding people to a late project can actually contribute toward its success. The "mythical man-month" (Brooks, 1978) tells us that if people are assigned to a late project, it will be completed even later. The reasons for a project being later are that at least one third of a persons time on a new project is taken up with learning, at least one third of the time of someone already producing on the project is lost to teaching the new person, and at least one third of the productive time of the project is used up by additional lines of communication due to more project members. Figure 9.10 shows the elements of Brook's law and how a project could be brought back on track without falling victim to the "mythical man-month" fallacy.

Elements of Brook's Law	How To Avoid Brook's Implications
1. 1/3 of a new person's time in initially lost to learning (the project, the people, the environment). 2. 1/3 of productive time from a current team member is lost to teaching the new member. 3. 1/3 of the time is lost to increased need for communication (if there are three people on a project there are three lines of communication, if four there are six lines – the equation is n x (n-1)/2.	1. Have current team members work overtime (limited). 2. Design the project in *incremental* fashion to avoid communications overload. 3. Keep potential project team members informed through status reviews so when you need them they can be productive quicker. 4. Reduce the deliverables (use a follow up project).

Actions for Brook's Law
Figure 9.10

Relationship Between Project Control and Planning

As stated earlier, a good project plan is needed for control to be possible. The quality of control is predicated on the reliability of predictions made during planning. Predictions involve skill, information, clarity of the work and deliverables, and the ability to account for unforeseen circumstances. Five elements of prediction relate to how effective controlling a project can be. These five are:

1. Skill of estimating (both major milestones and every activity)
2. Information about previous project efforts
3. Changes made to original requirements
4. Mistakes or "misreads" in identifying original requirements
5. Unforeseen circumstances

Managing these five elements will provide better control and less finger pointing about inevitable changes to original plans.

Skill of estimating is something every project manager wishes they could improve upon. There are ways to do it. One is to maintain an estimating database, and review current project estimates against the database. The database should contain each project's *problem orientation*, time durations on activities and/or milestones, information about the aspects and style of the project, major issues that came up during its life, and a primary metric. The metric for Information Technology (IT) development projects could be lines of code, or function points. During the control phase these estimates are checked against actual performance. If accurate enough, a Performance Indicator (PI) can be established for the remainder of the project. The PI is a factor that can be used to compute the remaining work, based on the work-to-date.

PI = Actual/Estimated

New Expected = (Previous Expected) x PI

PIs are more accurate if the project consists of homogeneous activities with similar estimating accuracies. Identifying and documenting tasks on a difficulty scale from easy to hard for future reference could prove valuable future estimating.

Change Control Budget

All excited, Linda and Frank went out to look at their new house under construction they discovered there was no way to enter the master bath from the master bedroom – the door had been overlooked during planning. Upon discovery they immediately called their head contractor and informed him. He said the change couldn't be made without substantial additional funds and a delay of about four weeks. "All for just a door" was Linda's response. It seems plumbing for the upstairs bath, as well as all the heating and air conditioning duct work for the second floor, was run through the only wall available for the door.

Projects that are approached *monolithically*, the waterfall model, need to have change control disciplines in place. In this approach requirements of the project's deliverables are defined at the beginning of the project like Linda and Frank's house. All the tasks to produce the deliverables are subsequently identified and arranged in the most productive manner. When changes occur after this plan starts to be carried out, project productivity suffers. The project manager needs a way to deal with these inevitable changes. When changes are initiated from the primary stakeholders, like Linda and Frank, the project manager needs a way to balance the need for the changes with the current schedule and budget. This is where a change control budget can help.

A change control budget can be fairly simple, or can be quite sophisticated. A "management reserve" is an example of a simple change control budget. It's used to charge against both the financial aspects of a project as well as the project's schedule for post-requirements definition changes. If Linda and Frank had a reserve, they could charge against it without impacting the overall expected cost or schedule of their house.

When, as a rule, there are no provisions made for changes, people estimating the work will overestimate because of the inevitable changes they've experience in the past. These overestimates are given various names such as cushion, pad, contingency, and fat. They really are misrepresentations of what the person really believes the particular task will need (baring no surprises). As a change discipline the pads can be removed for all tasks estimated in the project and added into a change budget for the entire project. The overall cost and schedule of the project is not reduced by the total of these pads but is included as a change budget for the entire project. Key stakeholders can then be informed the project will come in under cost and in less time if the change budget is not depleted. This puts the behavior for initially assessing the changes with the stakeholders (where it belongs), rather than with the project management hero trying to say "yes" to every change request. He/she can do this for a while because fat has been built into each estimated task.

Usage of pad/fat in project estimates builds into the project a learning disaster. People are learning all the time and you can't stop it. Honoring changes by our project hero because he/she built fat into the estimate, teaches that every change is possible. Teaching stakeholders to blindly expect all changes to be honored will meet with eventual disaster because more than likely not every change will be able to be covered by hidden fat in the estimate. Figure 9.11 shows the change budget created from padding.

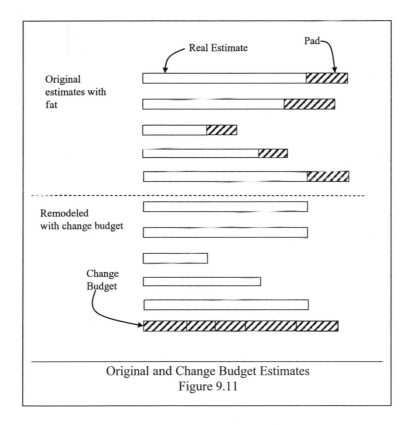

Original and Change Budget Estimates
Figure 9.11

The change budget acts as a buffer for the entire project and can be used to ward off changes in project budget and schedule yet still accommodate changes when stakeholders deem them worthy. The Theory of Constraints (TOC) uses a similar approach but uses multiple buffers at key project points (Goldratt, 1997).

"I Knew it All Along" Fallacy

Changes made to original requirements are inevitable, especially for large projects. Once stakeholders get a better sense of the project deliverables, they may see issues that are critical to the success of the outcome, and therefore need to be added after the project begins. If the *evolutionary* approach is taken, these sorts of changes are discovered in the natural course of project activities and the way it was planned -- re-planning will not be necessary. There is a common fallacy in human activity called "I knew it all along" (Nisbett, 1977). It has been shown through behavioral experiments that people will attribute more to their own knowledge of situations after they take place than they knew during its occurrence. Because of this fallacy it is difficult to tell if a requirement was actually missed and eventually revealed through a clearer understanding of the deliverable(s), or by falling victim to the "I Knew It All Along" fallacy. The concerned parties simply say they knew it but forgot to mention it.

This is a problem for next time because the one seeking requirements will assume those involved really do know all there is to know. These requirements seekers have learned those they seek requirements from have nearly perfect knowledge. They walk away with answers to the question: "Tell me what you need" thinking they have really been told it all. One approach to reduce this fallacy is to involve stakeholders in a review of a like project that mirrors some of the requirements. The similar project can function as a mental model and bring to mind requirements that may be missed. This is taking advantage of recognition versus recall. It has been shown that people are able to recognize elements much more readily than they are able to recall them without cues (Fiske, 1984). That's why most multiple choice tests are easier than fill-in-the-blank or essay.

Change Sources

Mistakes in identifying the original requirements can be made due to unavailability of the right people, inadequate communication process, or misrepresentation of the deliverables by others. When stakeholders, key to establishing the requirements, are unavailable, the project manager usually is left with a guess as to what is correct. If the key stakeholders are in a place of power in the organization (*autocratic* organization) then informal interactions with their lieutenants and/or office staff may help. Individuals who have learned how to "self-monitor" can use this kind of approach quite effectively (Goldman, 2002).

Inadequate communications, as a reason for changes, could be because there was not enough communication, or what was communicated was poorly understood. The best solution to this last issue is to document the communication in a short memo or email. This follow-up process provides a good audit trail for changes as well as confirming what was communicated.

Unforeseen circumstances can change original requirements for project deliverables. These circumstances could involve changes in the business such a mergers/acquisitions, changes in regulations, changes in competitive posture, or even changes in the way business processes are carried out (e.g. through Internet innovations). These kinds of changes require re-planning the project. If the original plan continues to be used as a baseline for control, the project is being control against the wrong expectations. It may be completed according to schedule, but the deliverables may never get used. If the changes are minor, within the original scope of the project, then re-planning may not be necessary but should be considered. If the project is planned at the activity level, and is being controlled at the activity level, re-planning of the activities may still be necessary even if the project is within scope because the activities may not be sequenced correctly.

Unforeseen circumstances cannot be overcome, but similar projects along with their environments can be used to assess the current project. The key question is what project is this one most like, and then review what happened to that project and others like it. This *outside view* reduces optimism inherent in most project plans, and brings a sense of reality to those plans (see chapter 8). Comparing the current project with others should be done throughout the project. It can provide an early warning the project is off-target.

PART FIVE

Projects and People

Good project managers can adjust their behaviors by intelligently assessing the people involved. Assessing others is a skill that can be developed and mastered. The next three chapters describe three topics that are a critical part of the assessment of people and their place on the project.

Managing a project to its successful completion involves getting things done with and through people. Managing and leading a project has three distinct roles. One is the *Manager* (M), next *Leader-1* (L1), and the other *Leader-2* (L2). These roles of management and leadership vary in their importance according to the project and its environment.

The *Management* (M) orientation means taking on the role of a logical assigner of resources across tasks, and/or to make sure that milestones are being completed on time, and/or even to ensure people have the kind of support needed for the project.

The *Leader* (L1) role involves being a proponent for the project to the external world. The project leader needs to be able to deal with political maneuverings, set up organizational areas for change that will come with introducing a new "way", and/or even to managing the impression others may have of the project and the people working on it.

The *Leader* (L2) role includes inspiring project people to accomplish the work in the best way possible and understanding them as people, rather than as automaton-type resources, and their motives for performing on the project.

Chapter 10

Project Authority

I remember one of my early encounters with authority outside the home. Before the sun had peeked over the horizon a door was flung open and loudly slammed against the wall. A voice could be heard at the volume of a train wreck. It was the drill instructor. We were arising to our first day of basic training (a.k.a. boot camp). One recruit still finishing his pleasant dream was removed from bed and shown the floor by the competent, if not loud drill sergeant. At that point no one in the opened bay barracks questioned the sergeant's authority. Actually his authority would not be questioned throughout the whole ordeal of basic training. How did the sergeant garner this authority? Where did it come from? Was it his rank, his control over our pay, his winning personality, his appearance, or maybe even his use of language?

Projects are not like military basic training, yet just as in basic training the person in charge of the project will need authority to carry it out (but usually not the kind of authority a drill sergeant displays). This chapter examines six sources of authority for the project manager. These six sources of authority are:

1. Formal
2. Financial
3. Bureaucratic
4. Technical
5. Identity (or charismatic)
6. Personality-dominance (also called Jedi mind-trick)

Multiple forms of authority are possible on any given project. Since many projects are changed mid-stream, it's a good idea to have more than one form of authority as a project leader. It's particularly true for those projects that may fall victim to a relative decrease in priority. In this case the project leader may lose whatever formal authority he/she may have had. Brief descriptions of the six forms of authority follow.

Formal

The word *formal* suggests this form of *authority* is related to or involving some formal structure, or associated with an official status for the project manager. *Formal authority* is meted out from someone who has it to give. *Formal* usually means someone within a power structure has issued authority to the project manger. It's a public granting and recognition of approval to carry out the project, and to get major stakeholders involved with minimum convincing. This form works well for those enterprises that are hierarchy-based command and control structures. It's safe to say our drill sergeant had at least this kind of authority since he got it from someone with the power to give it.

Projects that require significant stakeholder attention across an enterprise are served well by *formal* authority since it is usually well known and clearly communicated. Also, *formal authority* works best in contexts that are *autocratic* or *mechanistic* (see chapter 2). *Formal authority* may work against the project manager if the context is entrepreneurial or very innovative. In these contexts, projects are often run by homogeneous teams and hence honor equality among team players and not formally defined differences (see chapter 6).

Financial

When the project manager has *financial authority*, he/she may not have been formally announced as project manager, but does have financial/budgetary resources under their control. Someone with the proper status also gives this form of *authority*. Added duties with this form of *authority* may include financial budgeting, and reporting on the project as it unfolds. The following terms should be familiar to someone with this kind of *authority* (see chapter 9).

Related terms to be familiar with:
        BCWP – Budgeted cost to work performed.
        BCWS – Budgeted cost to work scheduled,
        S-Cost – A normal way to report cost on a project (cumulative cost)
        CBA – Cost-Benefit Analysis
        NPV – Net Present Value
        EVA – Earned Value Analysis

Project managers in enterprises that are *mechanistic* or *changing* from a *classical* production efficiency imperative to a *modern* imperative of service & quality, may find *financial authority* provides a great deal of leadership influence. Many traditional enterprises compete in their markets on low cost, while more modern enterprises have found ways to compete in differentiating their product/service in ways that appeal to customers in more ways than just cost (Porter, 1985). *Financial authority* is beneficial for projects that are based on cost-benefits and are intended to improve, through efficiency, processes within the enterprise. The mentality of decision making with these sorts of projects is usually based on a cost-based rationality of improvement. Even if the espoused notion is for quality, for *classical* enterprises, the projects are often funded on a "hurdle rate" measured through some form of cost-benefit analysis (see chapter 8). "Hurdle rate" is the minimum amount of return that is required before making an investment.

Bureaucratic

The word bureaucracy is based on Old French: *bureaucratie* : *bureau*, office; + *cratie*, rule. Enterprises, in order to be effective, need to integrate activities across their people and when this integration occurs a bureaucracy if formed.

In highly *bureaucratic* enterprises procedures are put in place in order to provide the coordination necessary for proper integration. For large and/or complex enterprises bureaucracies may seem to take a life of their own. Many activities are performed strictly for integrative purposes and not for their direct contribution toward the production of a product or service. While bureaucracies grow with the size of an enterprise, many modern enterprises have found ways to reduce bureaucracy by using technologies to simplify coordination and communication. *Traditional* enterprises that have a long history tend to be more bureaucratic since formalizing procedures gives the impression of efficiency. If the enterprise is *autocratic* or *democratic*, having *bureaucratic* authority can be very beneficial since they both require a high level coordination. To get something done in such an enterprise it may be important to know how to work through its size and structure. This is *bureaucratic authority*. On some projects a particular member may even be assigned the tasks of dealing with the bureaucracy.

The main point of this kind of *authority* is to know how to navigate the bureaucracy. This implies knowing the bureaucracy intimately, and being able to tell where, when, and to whom issues should be addressed.

Technical

Albert Einstein was respected and people listened to him, not because of any official title or deep understanding of how public communication takes place, but because of his technical knowledge. *Technical authority* consists of having special skills or practical knowledge especially in projects that are technical in nature. The more specialized the field the more this *authority* may be viable for the project leader. Communicating how elements of the technology (those caught within it – such as how a phone actually works) with how it performs requires an understanding of both the hidden or abstract parts and the visible tangible parts. This form of *authority* involves being able to connect the two components of technology – those that are real and those

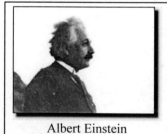

Albert Einstein
"Special relativity"

that are abstract (the visible and invisible). The project leader participates in technical aspects of the project and not just on its administration. This participation needs to be both visible and legitimate.

Some projects are technical in nature and exist in environments that honor one's technical knowledge. *Lassez-faire* enterprises are usually filled with people who are solving problems as independent groups. Leading projects in such environments usually requires one to be an equal member of the team in terms of knowledge and capability.

Other enterprises deal with traditional well-known technologies where the leader's technical knowledge is of little consequence. Several years ago an interview with a well-known and respected professional football coach produced the comment: "Professional football does not require geniuses like that Norman Einstein".

As a young film director Orson Wells, famous for the movie *Citizen Kane* and other endeavors, made what some critics say was a artful serious classic movie, but the movie lost its real place in history due to Wells' inattention. This movie, *The Magnificent Ambersons*, became a victim because Wells, director/project manager, left before it was really done. He thought he could do the editing from Mexico where he started work on another project, while spending many hours enjoying the party atmosphere. His technical creativity was lost because his attention was elsewhere instead of on the editing process so critical to a movie's creativity and flow. There will never be the artful, stylistic, classic directors cut of this movie because many of the original scenes were cut out and destroyed in Wells' absence (Carter, 2008). Technical authority is "hands on" and hard to maintain at a distance.

Orson Wells
Movie Director

Identity (or charisma)

George Herbert Mead is well known for his approach at understanding the *self*. In his approach the *self* is understood through ones ability to see oneself as others see us. To gain this perspective means to integrate all the viewpoints people have in a social reality of oneself into a representative example of "the other". I then understand myself from this "other" perspective. He identifies this as taking the role of the other to understand the *self*. If one can step back and realize this creation of the self is open to investigation, then its possible to adjust this "self perception" within the context of its social structure and then be able to self-manage.

Identity authority is a personal quality attributed to leaders who arouse fervent popular devotion and enthusiasm. This form of *authority* is sometimes referred to as charisma, personal magnetism, or charm. It's a skill that can be learned through devotion (Goffman, 1959). Someone displaying this form of authority knows how to read his or her audience and react appropriately to that reading. It is a matter of adjusting your style to match what would be most effect with the other(s) participating in the situation. Many good politicians rely on this approach to gain support from their constituency. It raises the level of identity across individuals by emphasizing common characteristics and reducing differences.

Requirements for good impression management:

> Have a setting that provides identity
> Assess the setting
> Have the correct props (e.g. style of dress)
> Be able to provide what is needed (skill of speaking in the right "language")
> Rehearsal (maybe)
> Take the position of the other – step into their shoes.

Many professional actors have learned to make their roles much more meaningful for their audiences by realizing what it would be like to actually be the person they are portraying. This could mean field research into the role, actually living in the environment the role is written in, or even personally picking the clothing to represent the role. It could also mean looking into oneself and finding experiences that mirror those of the role, and gaining an emotional confidence with the feelings (Stanislavski, 1936).

When a leader wants to identify with his or her audience two ploys can be used. One is to present a real true impression of their dominant self, being appropriately transparent about whom they really are. The other is to identify in some practical way with the audience interacting with an impression of oneself that fulfills expectations of the other(s). The first of these ploys is to "take me as I am" (see *Personality-Dominance* below), and the second is "I'll legitimately take you as you are". This second deals with impression management.

George Herbert Mead
"Take the role of the

Impression management, also referred to as self-monitoring (Snyder, 1987), as a way to achieve *identity authority*, is more than just a performance although performing is a part of it. People are usually much better at interpreting impressions than at giving them. They can identify when one comes from the "front", as a shallow surface level enactment, as opposed to one from the "back" where sincerity and who I really am resides. Two kinds of communication have been identified in this vain. One is about an expression given, and the other about an expression given off (Goffman, 1956). While they are both managed, a "back" performance brings with it a robust sense of all of the person, rather than a narrowly constrained picture. The "back" performer can connect to a "back" interpretation by the other resulting in a true impression. If the performers gain a sense of emotional confidence in the impression, and are sincere in its delivery, it becomes a legitimate exchange. It really does come from the "back". Most people can see through front performances, and can identify with back performances -- a critical step toward establishing *identity authority*.

A test of *identity authority* is to see if you can communicate something real in a transparent/"back" way with another person or a group that is/are acquaintance(s) rather than close friend(s).

The ideas of Emotional Intelligence (EI) also deal with *identity* authority. In EI four major points are made about how one manages themselves with others.

1. Personal awareness
2. Personal Control
3. Social awareness
4. Relationship management

Identity authority is using social awareness for self-control purposes. Evidence shows maturing in these four areas creates an increased ability to deal with others. Highly EI people are more likely to advance into executive level positions in many enterprises (Goleman, 2002).

Personality-Dominance (*Jedi Mind-Trick*) Authority

Imagine going to a meeting with a group you know quite well. You've been working with them for some time and have had many such meetings in the past. Everyone going into the meeting has their own reason(s) for being there, and are sincere about achieving a positive outcome (it may be solving a problem, assigning work, detailing an issue, etc.) One member of the group seems to be in the back of everyone's mind as everyone finds a seat around the table. They know this person may require special treatment by the group. The meeting is not about this person, nor does he/she possess any special qualifications for being there. Officially, he/she is simply a member of the group. No one acknowledges any special treatment toward this person, but it's an undertone of the meeting. At times the special treatment surfaces during the meeting, and at others no special treatment is evident. This person carries a kind of authority in the meeting that seems hard to explain.

This kind of *authority* is close to *identity authority* but its source is distinctly different. In *identity authority* the person adjusts their style to that of the receiving group (also referred to as self management or impression management). In *Jedi mind-trick authority* the person adjusts nothing in their way of acting. The person brings a personal strength that others have come to know. The strength may or may not be used in the meeting, but it's like an un-drawn gun. Its power goes to the possibility of behaving a certain way as well as to the actual behavior.

The basis for the *Jedi mind-trick authority* is two fold. One, the person has a dominant personality characteristic, and two, the person knows they have it and can manage it.

One of the most evident of these dominant personality characteristics is that of an objectionist also known as the Synthesist. The person brings in a problem solving strategy that is based on a dialectic approach. If the objectionist sees this situation as too far away from an acceptable group range for resolution, then he/she will attempt to draw everyone off on an extreme. This is being done in an attempt to find the place where any common agreement begins, then work toward an acceptable range (see Figure 10.1). Since the person knows they are realigning the group to an extreme (using their dialectic approach), it's not made in anger or necessarily trying to elicit an emotional response in others, though it may produce tension particularly for any new members of the group. The dominant personality trait being deployed maintains an aura of legitimacy and hence is given authoritative attention. Synthesis is one of five problem solving personality traits (Harrison and Bramson, 1982).

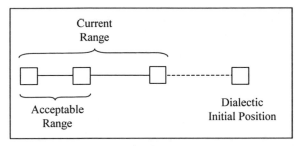

Dialectic Reasoning
Figure 10.1

The five problem solving traits useful for understanding *personality-dominance* authority are: synthesis, idealist, pragmatist, analyst, and realist (see Figure 10.2).

Personality Dominance	General Viewpoint	Description
Synthesist	Integrative	Speculative, challenges, change is good
Idealist	Assimilative	Relationships and values, being on same page
Pragmatist	Eclectic	Focus on outcome and what works
Analyst	Formal Logic	Method and plans, logically inflexible
Realist	Empirical/Induction	Based on facts and driven to concrete results

Personality Dominance Possibilities
Figure 10.2

Personality-dominance (or *Jedi mind-trick) authority* is personality strength (dominant trait) employed for the good of the group to reach its goal(s). The strength comes from using a personal problem solving strength. The elements of deploying *personality-dominance authority* are:

1. An issue or problem is presented to the group.
2. A person with a history of using a dominant personality characteristic within the group.
3. The trait used for the eventual good of the group's goal(s).
4. The person knows they have this trait and uses it when necessary.

If there is a real "trick" to this *authority* it is the person knowing they have this dominant trait and when it should be used. They come to know it by having successfully used it and/or by discovered it through personality testing. These tests include the Myers-Briggs Type Indicator®, Hemispheric Specialization, InQ, etc. They are commonly given in leadership training or personal improvement programs. One goal for these kinds of assessments is usually to appreciate the differences in others. The goal usually missed is how to apply or grow ones own strength. Testing is very powerful when taken seriously and used for self-examination of actual or possible strengths. Results are often a confirmation of what the individual already knows.

The ultimate personality strength is to be able to *transcend* ones own preferences (and strengths) to behave both as the situation demands and the people in it can accept. This comes through a maturity of practice and constantly trying to balance ones behaviors. Although this has a lot of earmarks to *identity* authority it's different. In identity authority the person adjusts their approach by "reading" the other, while in the transcendent approach the key is knowing when the situation calls for your strength or someone else's and adjusting your own behavior encouraging other behaviors and even changing the circumstances if possible. Figure 10.3 provides brief examples of people associated with certain forms of authority.

Form of Authority	Example	Comment
Formal	Drill Instructor	Given authority buy a hierarchical structure and willing to display this authority.
Purse String	Oskar Schindler	Nazi capitalist who saved Jews during WW II. People accepted his way because he paid them (bribes, etc.)
Bureaucratic	J. Edgar Hoover	Power in Washington circles due to a combination of personal secrets and his ability to work the system.
Technical	Ken Mattingly II	Apollo 13 grounded astronaut charged with solving a life threatening power problem on the returning damaged craft.
Identity (Charismatic)	Mikhail Gorbachev	As former president of the USSR he was able to adjust thoughts within and outside the republic.
Personality-Dominance (Jedi Mind-Trick)	Harry Truman	"Give-em hell Harry" was able to use his *realistic* personality strength to guide decisions on war efforts.

Authority Examples
Figure 10.3

Projects of Life – Purchasing an Automobile

This *evolutionary* project *begins* when you decide to purchase a new, or at least newer, automobile. Visiting many car lots reveals a wealth of interesting and appealing choices. The *end* of the project is when you take possession. Eight *basics* are important to any project but in this example from life the *leader basic* will be highlighted along with the *authority* parameter. Keeping oneself in the lead position during this project is critical to getting the best deal. Many people give up *leadership* because they feel they do not have the *authority* to complete the project. Many novice auto purchasers find this relieving since they have no desire to lead the project because they feel it is out of their hands anyway – they have no authority.

The six forms of authority are:
1. Formal
2. Financial
3. Bureaucratic
4. Technical
5. Identity (Charismatic)
6. Personality-Dominance (Jedi Mind-Trick)

One auto company secures the *leadership* position even before one considers a purchase. They make the purchase purely administrative with no haggling over price. They become the *leader* through *bureaucratic authority* because they know how to consummate the purchase and the buyer usually doesn't.

Other experiences show that *authority* for leadership moves from the purchaser to the seller because of *technical authority*. Many buyers do not know the technical part of automobiles and the seller uses this to capture the leadership role.

One way for the purchaser to remain the leader is to take advantage of the *financial authority* they have. Make sure funding is under your control by establishing it before beginning the search independent of the seller. This *financial authority* will keep you in the lead and provide both leverage in the deal and flexibility to move across purchasers. *Bureaucratic authority* is also available if purchasers can educate themselves using internet resources as to the value of the trade-in (if there is one) as well as the value of the auto to be purchased. This information is power in the purchaser's hands since the seller already has it and will use it to their advantage.

It's also worth noting that the seller often has *charismatic authority* – they will speak in the language of the buyer to make sure the buyer is comfortable and feel the seller is really "one of us".

While many auto purchasers are initially led by the buyer the *leadership* can switch (or be given up) to the seller due to time pressure and other resource constraints on the buyer. It may mean in the balance of all other things one has to do, the project may be best run by the seller. The buyer may just not have time to mess with it. Still "caveat emptor".

Chapter 11

Motivation on Projects

"Get something done" is a key tenet for every project manager. There are lots of activities that take up the project manager's day, but the importance of project productivity surpasses them all. On some projects getting something done involves little more than just knowing the goal and making sure an adequate amount of time and energy are expended toward reaching it. On other projects the effort to accomplish the goal may require marshaling special energy from a staff of people. The way one goes about this has often been labeled *motivation*. An oft-heard quote is "you need a motivated working team to really get things done". While true, it is only true some of the time, and most of the time the way one can go about this *motivation* depends on so many other variables many project leaders simply give up and resort to either the cattle prod approach or the cajoling, pleading, begging approach. Can a person be motivated? Is it true some people are self-motivated? Why are some people only motivated if attended to over a long period of time and given individualized well-metered attention? Good project managers know two things about *motivation*:

1. *When* to provide motivational interaction
2. *How* to provide motivational interaction

Motivational approaches should be taken on a project *when* the project and the people provide the opportunity. Projects have to allow motivational opportunities. If the project is too time constrained or the people are not subject to motivation (either psychologically or physically) attempting motivational approaches may work against "getting something done". *How* a project leader provides *motivation* is a function of an overall understanding and approach to *motivation*.

Providing a motivational interaction when needed is a sign of an effective leader, however *motivation* is not *leadership*, but a concept that pervades all roles within a project, and for that matter all of humanity. However, this discussion will be limited to *motivation* as it could take place on a project. In order to know how to motivate let's examine what is meant by motivation. Three alternative ways to think about project *motivation* are provided and are:

1. *Motivation* as a causal agent for action.
2. *Motivation* as experiencing a *place* that offers new opportunities for action.
3. *Motivation* as a learned disposition toward acting certain ways.

Motivation as a causal agent

If causation motivation is attempted, the project leader needs to do something that will directly cause the desired outcome. Included on the list of actions are such things as telling people how important the project is, assigning work that matches personalities, making sure the job contains motivational elements, stating clearly and plainly what is needed and when its needed, promising a financial bonus when completed, reminding people how important their job is to the company, taking them out to lunch, picking them up for work, hiring someone to do their laundry, giving them a cell phone, handing out hats/t-shirts, providing special dinners, playing good cop/bad cop with a cohort, giving a severe dressing down backed up immediately with a character building discussion, etc. These have all actually been used on projects. If applied blindly without some level of understanding about the projects and the people involved, you may end up expending a lot of work with little or nothing to show for it.

A story is told about Thomas Watson, founder of IBM, when he first started selling cash registers and failed. His boss, a successful man, called him into his office and severly chewed out Watson about his ineffectiveness as a salesman. His tone then changed and he began to tell Watson how to go about the job and that he personally would help him get better (Zientara, 1981). Watson soon became a most productive salesman, and he since used this motivational approach on others. For some individuals this works, but for others they

Thomas J. Watson
Founder of IBM

may take their marbles and play in another game. Motivation requires sensitivity to the situation and the people in it.

Figure 11.1 shows motivation as a causal act that leads to a motivational result where the person is not considered. Mediating influences explain differences in behavior/results that accompany the same motivating initiative.

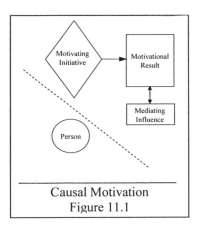

Causal Motivation
Figure 11.1

Three theoretical motivational approaches provide insight to a causal *motivation*. These three theories are: The two-factor theory (Herzberg), job design theory (Hackman and Oldham), and the extrinsic/intrinsic model (Deci) (Pinder, 1984). Each of these approaches assumes a causal agent produces resultant action.

In the Herzberg's two-factor theory each action or circumstance is interpreted either as a necessary condition for performance but not motivational, or optional for performance and potentially motivational. The necessary, but not motivational are called hygiene factors and include things we would consider normal expectations within the environment. For instance, at school you would expect to be provided seating. Having a seat does not motivate your behavior, but not having one may be de-motivating. These hygiene factors come from our learned expectation of what's normal. In other cultures the norms may change, and a desk may indeed be motivational – especially for people used to sitting on a dirt floor during class. In the normal business most people are provided opportunities to take a break from work. If workers are in an office a hygiene factor could be a place to sit or even a desk if the job "demands" it (see Figure 11.2).

Factors	Present	Absent
Hygiene	No impact	De-motivational
Motivators	Motivational	No impact

Hygiene and Motivator Factors
Figure 11.2

Motivators are those things that when provided lead to a preferred action. Motivators could include bonuses, special recognition, promotions, special meetings with the boss, etc. While not required to accomplish the work under normal circumstances these actions may increase motivated behavior. So the project leader needs to know the norms for their team in order to distinguish motivators from hygiene factors. Figure 11.3 shows this motivational model.

While visiting a steel mill, known as a mini-mill due to its small volume and usage of arc-furnaces to melt scrap metal, I was impressed by how fast everyone did their job within the mill. I expected to find grimy laden-down workers trudging through the day waiting for their shift to end. Instead I found a work crew that sprinted from one job to the next if it involved production, staying late to help the next shift keep things running smoothly, and having eyes that seemed to spark with enthusiasm. You'd think they were creating the next cure for cancer instead of making rebar steel (a low grade used for reinforcing cement). This had all the earmarks of motivated behavior. As it turns out they were paid bonuses for going over expected production quotas, and succeeded most of the time. Their increased income put these workers in the higher bracket of residents that lived in the community. Here was a plain instance of motivation <u>caused</u> by a reward system – both monetarily and socially.

When the norms are unknown people may be demotivated due to hygiene factors. One enterprise stopped purchasing pens and pencils assuming the employees should deem these instruments as part of their contribution to the work. Time and effort toward productive output was not enhanced by this move. While there are no numbers to back up the claim of lost productivity, time consumed by speaking with fellow-employees about the decision had productivity repercussions. This may be a minor example but in general once hygiene factors are in place removing them can be de-motivating. Motivation factors come from extra-ordinary inducements. These could be things, special attention, and reward structures such as bonuses at the mini-mill.

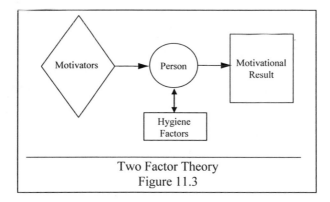

Two Factor Theory
Figure 11.3

Another similar approach is that of Hackman and Oldham. Motivation in this approach comes from the job design itself rather than things around the job. They postulate three critical psychological states, that if elevated, will lead to job-related motivated behavior, and that these psychological states can be manipulated by the way a job is designed. A job should be designed with five core job dimensions in mind: Skill variety, task identity, task significance, autonomy, and feedback. If the job is designed effectively with these five dimensions in mind, individuals in these jobs will experience meaningfulness, responsibility, and knowledge of results. Having these experiences will result in motivated behavior as shown by fewer turnovers, less absenteeism, high satisfaction with the work, and higher quality of work output. The causal agent in this instance is the job itself and how it's designed to produce the desired output (see Figures 11.4 and 11.5).

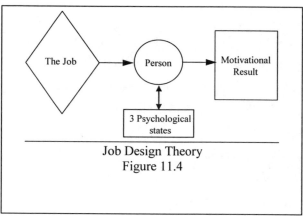

Job Design Theory
Figure 11.4

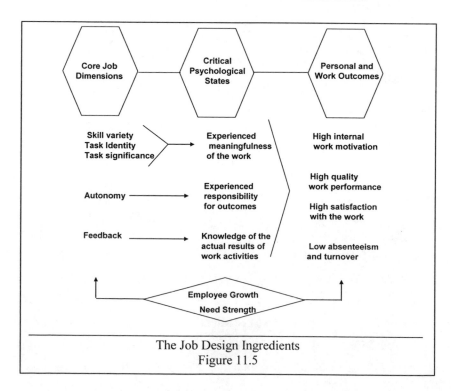

The Job Design Ingredients
Figure 11.5

Also, under a causal assumption, *motivation* can be interpreted through an extrinsic/intrinsic framework. With extrinsic conditions an external agent is the causal agent for motivational behavior. The external agent could be either some-thing or someone. Not only can things be extrinsic motivators but people can act as agents for *motivation* through organizational design (worker/boss relationships). Intrinsic *motivation* is provided from within the person. It's a self-induced way to initiate behavior. Intrinsic *motivation* has been associated with self-determination and growth needs. It's still basically causal in nature since the resultant *motivation* is caused by an environment that connects these desires or needs with the ability to act (see Figure 11.6)

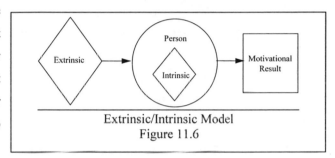

Extrinsic/Intrinsic Model
Figure 11.6

Results of extrinsic and intrinsic can be quite different. Having taught a special all day Saturday class for a number of years the way participants handle the morning snacks is revealing of extrinsic/intrinsic motivation. In classes where an individual independently begins bringing food for everyone, class members pick up on it and start bringing in other treats as well. In one particular class we had so many treats that lunch could have been skipped. In classes where they elect someone to be responsible for the treats (members collectively chip in to cover the cost), the treats were usually the same with little variety. Everyone was pleased with the result, but in the first instance where the motivation was intrinsic the resultant behavior was amazingly creative – and the food variety and quality was much better.

Causal agency for *motivation* is appropriate for projects that have clear expectations, endow the leaders with requisite authority and flexibility, and whose leaders have enough team insight to tell when a causal agent will be seen as motivational rather than manipulative (see *personality*-centered leadership in chapter 12). Project leaders' motivational actions are open to interpretation by those the actions are directed toward. Interpretations could be at the individual level, team level, or both. One could see giving t-shirts as a "cheep trick" or as a sign of how important the project team is in the eyes of the leader and/or the whole organization. If every team gets them and yours doesn't, it's a hygiene factor and hence could be a demotivator to your team. Causal incentives to act can result in motivated behavior as in the mini-mill example. Also, intrinsic motivation can in many instances encourage much more innovative behavior than extrinsic motivation as was evident in the Saturday morning food example.

Motivation As A Context/*Place*

Not everything is "caused", some things happen because the circumstances present opportunities and people take actions within the opportunities (Cohen, 1972). The causal assumption is built on reasoning that every act has a "firing pin" setting if off. While true for many actions it doesn't explain actions taken for their own sake. As an ultimate explanation, reasoning back to first causes for behavior may provide insight, but also may cloud explanations for some behaviors because these are better explained by their context of opportunity rather than a close connection to what happened before. Sometimes our circumstances can explain the motivated behavior much better than the immediately preceding events. I'm reminded of the note found by an owner of a car that was dented while parked on a busy street. The note read:

> I'm writing this note because there're a lot of people watching me and they knew I ran into your car. They would expect me to leave my name and contact information, but I'm not. Good luck!

Rather than a causal explanation, there can be a context, or *place*, explanation. Actions occur through the normal ebb and flow of life and may not inform the next best action or decision. *Motivation* in this view takes place in a context or *place* that embeds the action. Sometimes contexts can be devised that are motivational for those in it. For the project manager motivating individuals could invovle matching the context with the individuals allowing them to recognize their part and act accordingly (see Figure 11.7).

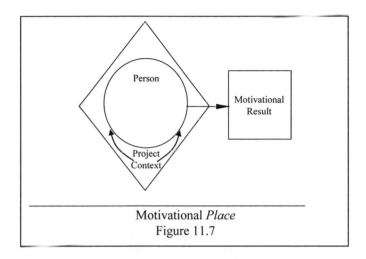

Motivational *Place*
Figure 11.7

When Goldilocks was looking for a good bed she found the one that's "just right" and proceeds to engage in the next natural act of sleeping. A *flow* state/place is an instance of this way of thinking about *motivation*. One experiences a *flow* state when the behavior is engaged in for its own sake – the actions needed are in a *context/place* the individual finds "just right" (Csikszentmihalyi, 1990). Many people with hobbies get lost in their *flow* states, and time loses its absolute value – one may look up at the clock and say, "I wonder where those last two hours have gone". This also happens at work when project workers are aligned according to their preferred job. The project leader should look for flow opportunities, and recognize them when they're occurring. This will reveal how a person can be motivated by the right *context/place*. One job for the project manager is to protect the context for these motivated workers. This may involve having a separate site for the team, removing phones, or even handling their mundane tasks that might interrupt their *flow*, like ordering lunch in.

In the job characteristics approach, the "job dictates the person's behavior", in the context/*place* approach "the person resonates with the job". Or another way to look at it is the job does not exist as it should without the person. The person is a key ingredient for motivation in this approach.

In the *context/place* approach motivation is not caused by specific acts by the project leader, but brought about by placing people in their best motive *context/place*. It's not whether there are outside influences, or self-generated influences to behavior, but only behavior in the moment with its own self-referent reason to be motivational (DeCharms, 1983).

With this motivational approach the job for the project leader is to be sensitive to a person's *place* within the whole and help them find it. Once accomplished, more motivated behavior will ensue. For the project manager it's both a feeling and a thoughtful awareness.

Motivation As Learned Dispositions

One approach to *motivation* highlights four general learned motive dispositions (McClelland, 1985). These dispositions are learned over time through a variety of life circumstances. The four motive dispositions are *achievement, affiliation, personalized power*, and *socialized power* (see appendix B for a motive disposition assessment instrument).

Motive dispositions are a recurrent orientation toward a goal state that drives and orients behavior. While this may sound causative these motive dispositions are learned tendencies to act and not an explanation for every act. Dispositions are created by past experiences of demands in the environment being matched with appropriate incentives. The demand-incentive connection is how a disposition is continually learned. When a circumstance presents the opportunity (or demand) for a disposition to be aroused a tendency to react will occur. The tendency will be one toward the need to *achieve* (overcome an internal goal of excellence), a need for *affiliation* (participate in a relationship with another), a need for *personalized power* (hold the environment captive for your own will), and/or a need for *socialized power* (bring the environment under some control for the good of those in it) (see Figure 11.8).

Motive Disposition	Main Idea	Project Opportunity
Achievement	Overcoming internal goal	Sticky technical problem
Affiliation	Relationship with other(s)	Schedule and coordinate project meetings
Personalized Power	Control for the good of the self	One person rules due to their expertise.
Socialized Power	Control for good other others	Organize stakeholder participation groups

Dispositional Motives
Figure 11.8

A project manager can discover motivational needs and design the project opportunities according to these needs. Some projects will not fit this approach because they're either too small or are too narrowly defined to permit a flexible motivational approach. If there's a part of the project that presents a sticky technical problem, someone with both the ability and a high need for *achievement* would be good to tackle it. If a part of the project required heavy stakeholder interaction, then it would be good to get someone involved who understood the particular stakeholder knowledge area, and who has a high need for *affiliation*. If part of a project needed someone to organize the stakeholders into more participative groups then a person with a high need for *socialized power* would be a good candidate for the job.

The job of the project manager is not to change motive dispositions, but to recognize them and interact accordingly. The motive disposition way of dealing with *motivation* on a project requires the project manager to have a significant history with the individuals or develop one during the first part of the project. The manager needs to know of their *achievement, affiliation, socialized power*, *personalized power* dispositions. Plus, of course, the project needs to have a variety of opportunities so individuals can be matched with their motive dispositions (Ferratt, 1986). The major distinction in this motivational approach is the feedback loop involved in learning (see Figure 11.9).

For instance, if a team member was high in need for *achievement*, assigning them a task with a moderate to high level of difficulty would be motivational. Another team member may be high in need for *affiliation*, so assigning them more stakeholder interaction tasks would be motivational for them. Get these two mixed up and you have two team members not performing at their best.

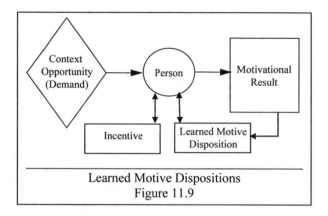

Learned Motive Dispositions
Figure 11.9

Motivational Role of the Project Leader

One way a project leader can be more effective is to assess which motivational assumptions should be dominant for leading the work. Project characteristics are shown in Figure 11.10 to indicate which assumption may be the most beneficial to employ.

Motivational Assumptions	Project Goals	Project Length	Project Team
Causative	Clearly Specific	Short (1-6 months)	Hand picked
Place	General	Medium (6–12 months)	OK
Dispositions	To be made specific	Long (over one year)	Who you have

Motivational Assumptions and Project Characteristics
Figure 11.10

Suppose you are the project manager for a two year project and are assigned 20 people for most of the project. Using the *dispositional* motivation approach could prove most beneficial. Assign the interface activities to those high in need for *affiliation*, the complex and difficult activities to those high in need for *achievement*, and the coordination activities to those high in need for *power*. Of course people are much more complex than just their motivational proclivity, so the project manager needs to consider the whole person when making assignments. The motivation approach is just one tool to assist in making such assignments.

Chapter 12

Leadership

Abraham Lincoln, a great leader from many perspectives, was able to lead through varied situations; from the strategic decision to have General McClelland destroy Lee's army after the Battle of Sharpsburg, to not holding General McClelland accountable for his lack of action to do so. The General just came through the bloodiest battle in American history, and whether he, nor his troops, could emotionally carry out the order to attack the trapped Lee. Lincoln being sensitive to this human situation let this pass and kept McClelland in power. However, later after other near insubordinate issues with McClelland Lincoln removed him. Lincoln's sensitive, egoless, humble, and force of will leadership style is emblematic of a great project leader.

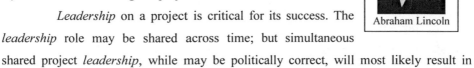

Abraham Lincoln

Leadership on a project is critical for its success. The *leadership* role may be shared across time; but simultaneous shared project *leadership*, while may be politically correct, will most likely result in problems for the project. Decisions will take longer, people will be confused about whom to approach about issues that will inevitably surface during the project, and reporting on the project will be inconsistent. Yet on some projects having two leaders, one from a major stakeholder area and the other from the group that produces the project deliverable, may be the difference between success and failure particularly if active stakeholder participation is needed but difficult to obtain.

<u>Ability and Status</u>

Project *leadership* is an ability that individuals can acquire or perhaps be born with, but it's also a status individuals can have. The best situation is to have both the ability and status. Status is acquired from other people. Status could be granted by someone with the requisite power to do so, or from a group of people that collectively give it. Status is granted to those that have the *authority* to lead. There's more than one way to garner *authority* on a project, and the prudent project manager should assess their own *authority* as understood by members of the team and external stakeholders (see chapter 10).

Distinctions between *management* and *leadership* reveal these as separate roles (Kotter, 2001). Management is concerned with stewardship of resources to meet plans. *Leadership* is twofold. One, *leadership* is about strategic influencing, and second, leading people to act at an individual level. Hence management/leadership has three distinct roles – management, leadership for strategy, and leadership for individuals.

Dwight Eisenhower provides a good example of these three leadership roles. When he was making the decision to launch D-Day activities he was perhaps the most powerful leader in the world. He, with the help of many others, had devised a plan that had to be agreed on by multiple parties. One of his jobs as a leader was to communicate and sell this plan to the stakeholders. Once the decision was made to "go" his role of leader became one of manager – making sure troops were supplied with what they needed. Also, the primary leadership role for the war switched to the field officers, lieutenant and captains, to lead their troops into battle.

Dwight Eisenhower

The three generalized worldviews provide a baseline for three leadership roles and the abilities it takes to function in these roles. The worldview of *strategy* concerns seeing the big picture and how individual projects fit into it (L1-role). This leadership role involves marshaling resources, gaining project acceptance, and constructing a vision for the project. Outcomes of this form of leadership are clear objectives, well defined approval processes, a solid overall guiding strategy for the project, and appropriate participation of opinion leaders and advocates. Eisenhower performed this role by selling his plan to the critical stakeholders. The worldview of *machines* implies the leader is focused on productivity, processes, acquisition and optimal utilization of resources, as well as the balancing of cost and time constraints of the project. This is a management leadership role (M-role). A worldview of *people* ascribes to the leader a primary concerned for progress from individuals as persons (L2-role). Leadership while an aspect for an individual has social components especially on projects. The social context is more than a backdrop; it plays into the way a leader leads. This form of leadership consists of mentoring individuals, and making sure the team maintains a sense of direction for the project.

When project leaders make worldview mistakes it's usually evident. One common mistake is to assume the project's objective (established from the world of *strategy*) will suffice for moving the people toward action in obtaining it. Often the team members understanding of the objective is not sufficient to produce hard work. They may require a more personal leadership approach (L2). For instance an L2 approach to initiating a project would be to call a meeting of the team to get their feedback on the current plan and how they might see it unfolding.

Leadership/motivational research attribute performance to human relationships, as well as the setting of reasonable goals. The human relationships piece is important because each person may have differing difficulty levels for realistic goals (e.g. a high need-for-achiever will opt for more difficult rather than more conformable goals – see chapter 11). The tangible result, or objective, of a project can contribute to team cohesion but should not be relied upon as the sole reason for effort. People work for their own reasons and meeting the project objective may not be one of them. For project teams itching to apply their various talents to the project, leading the team with comments about the project's ultimate objective may not be helpful, and may even hinder progress.

All three forms of leadership may be required on a project, and the issue for the project manager is to decide when to perform which role. As the project unfolds these leadership needs may vary. Good project leaders should consider what balance of leadership is required of the project taken as a whole. The predominant requirement may be to balance activities and people, or to lead according to the human nature of the team, or to communicate to major stakeholders to both sell the project and sustain it (e.g. keep it funded) (see Figure 12.1).

The three forms of project leadership are shown in Figure 12.2. One section of the triangle of project leadership may be more important than another given the project circumstances (Browdy, 2007).

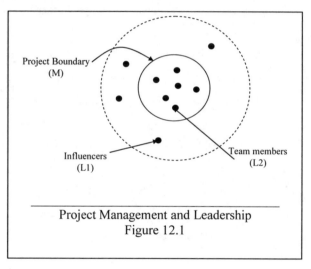

Project Management and Leadership
Figure 12.1

Models of Leadership

Developing the ability to function in one of the three roles of project leadership means having a way to think about that role, a model, and a way to master the model. Three models are presented below. Two are two dimensional leadership models, and one a personality model. One of the two dimensional models is for the machine world (the M-role),

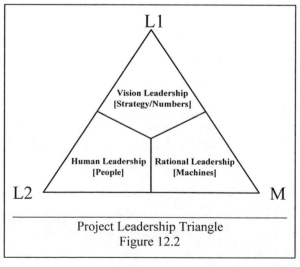

Project Leadership Triangle
Figure 12.2

the other two dimensional model is for the *strategy* world (L1-role), and the personality-based approach for the people world (L2-role).

Situational Leadership® Model

The Situational Leadership® model is good for understanding and leading in the *machine/process* world identified as the management role (M-role) of project leadership (Hersey, 1988). It also deals with the world of people, but primarily as people are understood to impact task accomplishment. The two dimensions in this model are *task* and *relationship*. Key to this model is that leaders need to assess the readiness of their followers for a task and apply a leadership style that best fits the situation – balancing the person in the situation. This means developing a capability to assess followers and make the appropriate adjustments to get task performance. The prevailing duty of this leader role is to see that tasks are performed that meet specific and/or general project plans. The Situational Leadership® model provides an approach that connects tasks with those who have to perform them. The two-fold demand on the M-role is to know the tasks to be accomplished, provided by good planning, and to provide leadership guidance. Four ways to apply leadership guidance according to the model are: *delegating, informing, selling,* and *participating* styles of leadership.

Emphasized in this model are individual differences across situations and enacting the leadership style that matches the situation. On the *task* dimension leadership is concerned with the task to be performed. These tasks could include writing computer programs, balancing the books, or even digging a ditch. *Task* leadership behavior is assisting either directly or indirectly, in the performance of the task. *Relationship* leadership behavior is about supporting the person in accomplishing the task though encouraging comments, setting agendas, as well as making the follower feel secure and confident in accomplishing the task. When there is low relationship and low task leadership required a *delegating* style is used, with high task and low relationship it's *informing* (or *telling*), with high task and high relationship it's a *selling* style, and with high relationship and low task the leadership style is *participating* (see Figure 12.3).

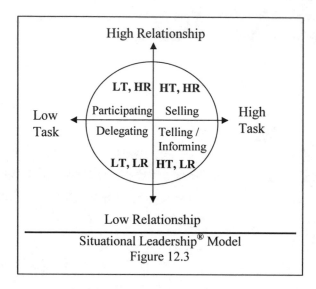

Situational Leadership® Model
Figure 12.3

As an example of this model suppose there's a status review meeting scheduled in which one of your direct reports on the project needs to make a presentation. This person knows all about what should be presented, but has never made a presentation to a group of managers before. They do not need task support from the leader, since they know what to present, but they do need relationship support to get them comfortable for making the presentation. The leadership style called for is *participating*. You could image another scenario where the person is quite confident in making the presentation and knows what to present. The leadership style called for in this case is *delegating*.

Leadership in this model is situational since the same person may require another leadership style from one task to another. The key to using this model is assessing the followers' need for leadership across the two dimensions of task and relationship, and then adjusting the leadership style to meet the need for the person performing the task.

The Dimensional® Model

The Dimensional® Model is good for dealing with the world of strategy –L1 leadership. This two-dimensional leadership model deals with how dominant (or submissive) another person is as well as how warm (or hostile) they are (Lefton, 2000). Results are four possibilities for both the leader and the other person. The four are dominant and hostile, passive and hostile, warm and hostile, and dominant and warm. The idealistic leader, in the model, can maintain a dominant/warm approach no matter what kind of behavior the other person is displaying. This is often referred to as the Q model of leadership where Q1 is dominant and hostile, Q2 is passive and hostile, Q3 is passive and warm, and Q4 is dominant and warm (see Figure 12.4). This model is good for a leadership role that requires influence in any environment (the *strategy* world). It can be used in any situation, and once Q4 is mastered, applied to any stakeholder.

What makes this model particularly suited to the *strategy* world (L1 leadership) is its emphasis on assessing people on an emotional/strength grid along with their position within the enterprise. For project managers this could be anyone from top executives to subordinates. Dealing with project stakeholders outside the project requires one to adjust to their emotional-strength position about the project. Some people will see the project as the last thing they really want to participate in thus elevating their emotional component of any communication. Adjusting to their position allows the project manager to effect the communication in a way that is acceptable to the other person. When such adjustments are not made a shouting match may ensue, the silent treatment given, or even passively agreeing to everything with no intent to act on the agreements. When situations are elevated to an emotional crescendo people will more often than not revert to their most natural behavior rather than the behavior that may lead toward a resolution. This model, if appropriately used, will give the project manager a way to rise above the situation and maintain a Q4 position even during the worst of interactions (see Figure 12.5).

Of course the model is also useful in the world of people, however it does not consider their personality, nor their motivational issues outside of a "what's in it for me" approach. It's strength is being able to size up people and communicate with them effectively no matter their position with the organization. If leadership is not required at the personality level (L2) then this approach may be all that is needed.

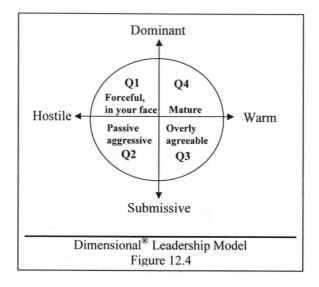

Dimensional® Leadership Model
Figure 12.4

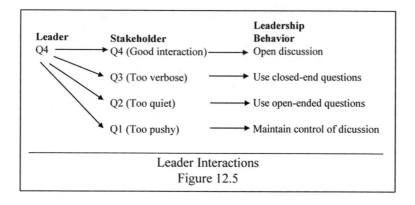

Leader Interactions
Figure 12.5

Personality-Based Leadership

This is a *people* worldview of leadership (L2). A leadership approach that relies on ones own personality comes from Carl Jung and his concepts of personality and the *self*. This leadership approach is also about being able to assess the other person, and relies on the appreciation of differences. Recognizing the *self* in others (their personality) will allow the leader to understand the world of human interactions. This leadership model is good for project teams because the team members can learn to integrate their respective preferences by understanding a variety of personalities. A group of people may not be a team, but may become one by understanding their various personalities and how they might work together with them.

Carl Jung's ideas have been popularized in many business communities through the usage of the Myers-Briggs Type Indicator® (MBTI®) (Myers-Briggs, 1980). The MBTI® is a cognitive test that assesses personality. It's based on Jung's psychology of opposites, individual processing of information about the world, and a maturity of the *self*. Maturing comes by overcoming biases of opposites through a process of alter-ego appreciation resulting in transcendence. Personality-base leadership is an appreciation and understanding about the particular implications for integrating various personalities into a well-functioning team. With the idea of opposites the leader recognizes that not all people are the same, and as a matter of fact, they differ along several dimensions. In the MBTI® four dichotomous dimensions are measured resulting in 16 different personality types. The four dimensions are:

1. Introvert / Extrovert (how we prefer to interact with the world around us)
2. Sensing / Intuition (how we prefer to gather information)
3. Thinking / Feeling (how we prefer to make distinctions with information)
4. Perceiving / Judging (what we prefer to do about information)

Leadership can be seen as an aspect of the *self* and independent of other aspects such as thinking/feeling. When a leader can recognize their own personality, both for what it is, and what it is not, then it's possible to apply personality characteristics to other types of personalities. Maturity of the *self* is a process that comes to appreciate the opposite along each dimension. Once this is learned then the individual has transcended their limits and can identify with all possible personalities. With this appreciation comes the capability to lead any collection of people. A project leader then is someone who can interact with anyone, and when doing so, interface with other personalities in such a way to produce a high level of social influence. With this in mind, the greatest value of the MBTI® is to gain an insight into opposites, and learn to appreciate the struggle within the *self* to resolve inconsistencies. Seeing the inconsistencies in others, and their struggles, is a leadership capability that is displayed in highly charged and malleable social situations (see Figure 12.4). The introvert does not see the value in extroversion unless he/she considers it as also what they are in some way. The fact that an introvert can be extroverted frees the personality from it cage and opens understanding of other people as they really are.

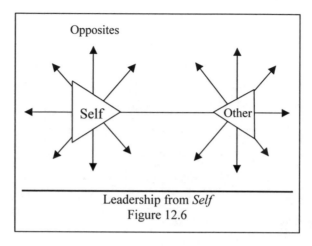

Leadership from *Self*
Figure 12.6

When diagnosing team personality problems the Jungian model is very powerful. It can suggest who may prefer what jobs, why some people find it hard to get along with others, and when to attribute personality conflicts in situations rather than simple task abilities. This sort of leader (L2-role) also has the responsibility for communicating to individuals how personalities are different, and resolve personality conflicts through their individual self-awareness.

People who realize transcendence (overcoming ones own personality type) may be identified by the reflective statements they make about others. This is an indicator they're thinking about how other people behave, or having realized their preferences how to interact with them accordingly. Such statements may be:

> *The purposes of a man's heart are deep waters, but a man of understanding draws them out.*
> Proverbs 20:5

> Sometimes you just have to understand how she deals with people. She's like that.

> He's just an old fart and hard to get along with, but when you get to understand him he can teach you a lot.

An Alternative Leadership Approach Based on Jung's Psychology

Jung's theory also provides insight into another concept of leadership. We hold opinions or preferences about leadership itself and these preferences set the stage for how we lead as well as how we react to other leaders. Jung's approach gives us access to these various leadership preferences. This framework for understanding leadership is based on Jung's idea of opposites, integration of multiple dimensions to reveal a preference, and transcendence (our ability to overcome these personal preferences).

People vary on how they think about leadership. Some see it as predominantly a *Social* (So) phenomena, while others see it as *Formal* (F). In this approach to leadership both these aspects are part of every leadership preference. Individual preferences may tend to more *Social* than *Formal* or vice versa. Some people may hold these preferences much stronger than others, and lead predominantly according to these preferences. The So/F dimension is one of three and is foundational for the other two (see Figure 12.5, the So/F distinction is similar for a leadership preference as the MBTI dimension of *perceiving* and *judging* is for preference concerning what to do about information – that is preference for *sensing/intuition* over *thinking/feeling* dimensions respectively).

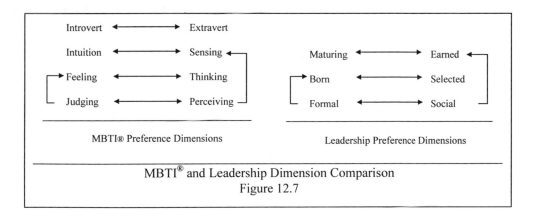

MBTI® and Leadership Dimension Comparison
Figure 12.7

A Social (So) preference is refined along a So dimension of opposites from Maturing (M) to Earned (E). Maturing leadership preference indicates the person sees leadership as something they can mature or grow into where the energy and primary unit of growth is within the individual and their capability to interact with their social world. The Earned (E) preference indicates that leadership capability is not within the person but within the social order itself. It's when people recognize the person as a leader that leadership takes place. This has been referred to as followership (Hollander, 1970). In this preference the person considers leadership as something earned from the social group by the group awarding credits to the leader.

The Formal (F) leadership dimension consists of Born (B) and Selected (Se) opposite preferences. In the Born preference people believe that leaders are Born to become a leader and that every occurrence in life is just one more opportunity to engage this natural ability. This preference views leadership as formally given at birth by their creator, DNA, etc. The Selected (Se) preference is also formally given but by someone else. The other person has formally selected the leader (see *formal* authority).

With three dimensions and two possibilities for each dimension, there are eight possible leadership preferences (see Figure 12.6). It's interesting to note that each person has their own leadership preference type; organizations also have a preference type that may or may not coincide with individuals in the organization. In this mismatch situation if people are not able to transcend their type they may not be able to work effectively. This is also true of project teams where the team individuals do not share the leadership preference of the project manager (or major stakeholders). This is a challenge for the project manager to transcend their leadership preference for the benefit of a well-functioning team and a successful project.

FMB Aristocratic leader	FMSe Benevolent Dictator	FESe Scout leader	FEB Commander
SoMB Driving leader	SoMSe Mentor leader	SoESe Empathic leader	SoEB Godfather

Leadership Preference Types
Figure 12.8

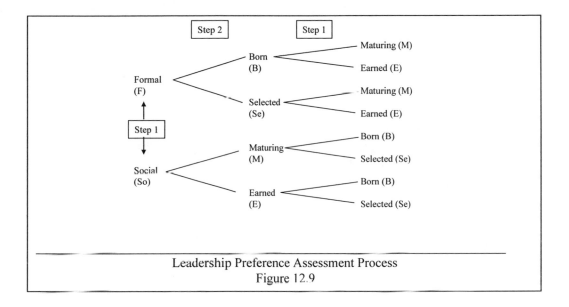

Leadership Preference Assessment Process
Figure 12.9

A classification process can be used to determine leadership preference for oneself and others. Figure 12.7 can be used to assist in this three step process. First is to decide if the leadership preference displayed is *Formal* or *Social* then proceed to examine the other two dimensions. As examples, let's look at General Patton and Mohandas Gandhi. First, is General Patton *Social* or *Formal*? His behavior as well as other evidence suggests his preference would be *Formal*. Consequently, then decide his preference along the *Formal* dimension of either *Born* (B) or *Selected* (Se)? *Born* is most likely since he has been quoted as saying he was born to lead men into battle. Finally his *Social* dimension is considered (his weak dimension). It is either *Maturing* (M) or *Earned* (E). Since he earned his military rank he must have displayed behavior that revealed his preference for *earned* over *maturing*. His leadership preference identifier is FEB (Commander). With Gandhi we conclude that he was a *Social, Earned, Selected* leader – SoESe (Empathic leader). Figure 12.8 highlights characteristics of the dimensions used in assessing leadership preferences.

Dimension	Characteristics
Social **So**	Contribution through wisdom Relates ideas that matter to the whole group Gauges popular opinion
Maturing **M**	Self-improvement Mentors others Has inquisitive dialogs
Earned **E**	Validation by followers Seeks opinion from subordinates Includes the group
Formal **F**	Honor from the position Uses well defined channels of communication Follows official directives
Born **B**	Self reliance Displays confidence Makes decision on their own
Selected **Se**	Organization structural clarity Assigns work effectively Takes a "win/lose" approach

Leadership Preference Dimension Characteristics
Figure 12.10

Summary

In the Situational Leadership® model a leader's behavior should be adjusted according to the situation, where *leadership* applies to both a person and their performance on a task. In the Dimensional® model one is expected to manage from a Q4 position (dominant and warm). Just as in Situational Leadership® this model requires the leader to assess followers but here according to their Q quadrant. Once the assessment is made the leader can then proceed in an individualized way. Leading a Q2 will be different than leading a Q3.

A personality-oriented *leadership* approach is how the leader, as a person, possesses within the *self* a mature personality that others recognize and accept on a personal level. The personality-based leaders possess capabilities that allow them to react to other people in ways these people understand, while simultaneously growing themselves through such interactions. These interactions personally enlighten and teach them something about themselves – who they are and who they are not. Leading other people through a personality approach is more like a dance where the partners are different and interacted with individually through understanding their personalities and leadership preferences.

Leadership on projects involves knowing yourself and knowing all the stakeholders, both the project team and all those external to it, so that effective communication can take place and things get done. Projects exist in multiple worlds: The worlds of *strategy, machine,* and *people*. Balancing these three worlds is key to leading a project effectively. Knowing a project requires a lot of *L2* a little of *L1* and some of *M* leadership approaches should signal which leadership tool(s) is best. Being flexible at leadership is needed because from one project to the next leadership demands may change.

PART SIX

Project Parametric Analysis

The parametric analysis is a way to think about how to manage projects – this is different than defining or determining exactly how to go about managing a project. The parametric analysis in chapter 13 can help by using the parameters described in the earlier chapters and applying them to a specific project. It can also help in a more powerful general way. It is a way for any project manager to improve on their performance by mastering the general parametric model.

A next step is to make the general model more personal by modifying the parameters to fit ones own environment (chapter 14). Subsequent projects can then be used to refine this personal model even further.

The practice of mastering the general model, building a personal model, and then continually refining it describes the sorts of things one does to become a project management master.

Chapter 13

Conducting a Parametric Analysis

From one perspective we could say that people have been managing projects all their lives. From birth to death consider our lives as a series of projects. Even as youngsters. For instance in the movie *A Christmas Story* the young boy sets out with the objective of getting a BB gun for Christmas. The eight basics of a project are present for the BB gun project and the boy finds ways to deal with them. Even when the lad's parents were planning his birth they were engaged in a project. Passing from one grade to the next in school is a project, getting a job, retiring, and finally funerals could be considered a project.

The "projects of life", as mentioned above, are a lot like playing pitch and catch in the backyard in hope of mastering the game of softball. A practice field is really needed for softball, and the same is true for mastering project management. The practice environment for project management is the parametric analysis. It gives the hopeful project manager master access to the key ideas of every project. Practice is also possible by applying the parametric analysis to as many projects on which one can gather information.

The parametric analysis is also valuable when a project is first getting underway by providing an initial understanding. If the project manager just completed a project *exactly* like the current one, then knowing how to manage the project would be a piece of cake. Since this is not possible, ever, we need a place to start from scratch to assess the project. Once part of the assessment is completed it may be possible to find a similar project, and go from there. The analysis starts with the broadest, primary parameters, and proceeds from there (see Figure 13.1).

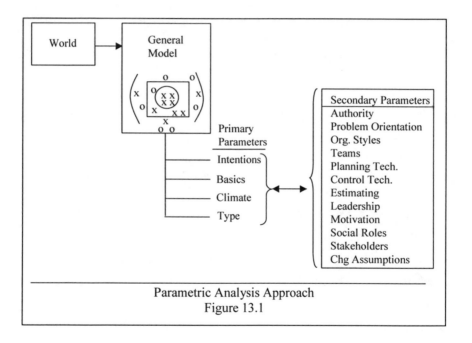

Parametric Analysis Approach
Figure 13.1

The result of a parametric analysis reveals which parameters are most relevant for achieving success. The process involves an examination of the secondary parameters given one knows the values of the primary parameters (e.g. knowing the value of the *intentions* parameter is *strategic*). The goal is to see which secondary parameters really matter for the project – which ones are "in play". Both an algebra for parametric analysis and a cell format will be used. The algebra is shown in Figure 13.2, and is provided so that shorthand notation can be used to go beyond the rudimentary but revealing initial parametric analysis.

The four primary parameters should be used to provide an initial assessment of the project. Once values or the primary parameters are established, the secondary parameters are revealed (see Table 13.1).

PM = <INT, BAS, ORC, PTY, AUT, PRO, ORS, TEM, PLT, CTT, EST, LDR, MOT, SOR, STA, ASP>

Where:

PM = Project Management

Primary Parameters
INT   = Intentions
BAS   = Basics
ORC   = Organizational Context
PTY   = Project Types

Secondary Parameters
AUT = Authority
PRO   =Problem Orientation

ORS   = Organizational Style

TEM   = Teams

PLT   = Planning Techniques

CTT   = Control Techniques

EST   = Estimating

LDR   = Leadership

MOT   = Motivation

SOR   = Social Roles

STA   = Stakeholder Communications

ASP   = Change Assumptions

Parametric Algebra for Project Management
Figure 13.2

PM = <INT, BAS, ORC, PTY>

          Intentions   = <Experimental, Process, Strategic, Cultural>
            Basics   = <Beginning, End, Objective, Leader, Staff, Resources, Quantitative, Research, Other Projects>
Organizational Context = <Autocratic, Democratic, Lassez-faire>;
                               <Classical, Modern, Changing>;
                               <Mechanistic, Organic>
        Project Types = <8> … based on requirements clarity (Structure), Technology, and Size

Identify which is the predominant intention for the project.

Intentions			
Experimental	**Process**	**Strategic**	**Cultural**

Identify which basic(s) are missing or weak.

Basics								
Beginning	**End**	**Objective**	**Leader**	**Resources**	**Quant.**	**Research**	**Other Projects**

Identify the context(s) of the project.

Decision Making Context			Supply Demand Relationship			Enterprise Performance	
Autocratic	**Democratic**	**Lassez-Faire**	**Classic**	**Modern**	**Changing**	**Mechanistic**	**Organic**

Identify the type of project (based on aspects of size, structure, and technology).

Types							
1 HS,LT,L	**2** HS,LT,S	**3** HS,HT,L	**4** HS,HT,S	**5** LS,LT,L	**6** LS,LT,S	**7** LS,HT,L	**8** LS,HT,S

      HS = High Structure
      LS = Low Structure
      HT = High Technology
      LT = Low Technology
      L = Large
      S = Small

Primary Parametric Analysis
Table 13.3

What follows is a step buy step approach for conducting the parametric analysis (see Figure 13.4). Each of the primary parameters (*Intentions, Basics, Context, Type*) are reviewed and used to decide which of the secondary parameters are "in play" (receive a vote toward identifying them as a key parameter). To conduct the analysis the project manager needs to know enough about the project to identify the values for the primary parameters. So before conducting a parametric analysis some project discovery legwork will be needed.

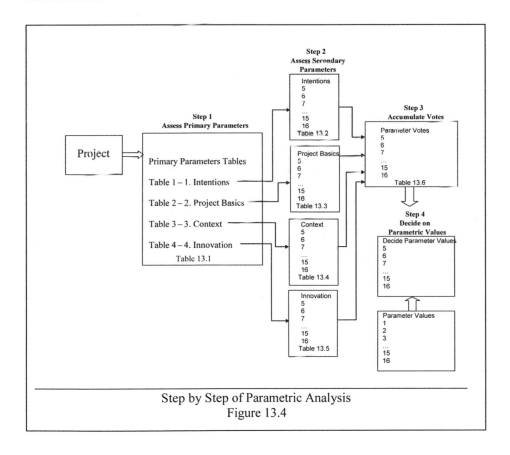

Step by Step of Parametric Analysis
Figure 13.4

Intentions Assessment

Given a certain *intention* only some of the secondary parameters should be considered important (this is independent of any particular project). Reasoning, not included here, reveals that every one of the four project *intentions* should include considerations for the secondary parameters of *authority, problem orientation, teams,* and *change assumptions* (they're kept in the game). Projects with a *process* intention should also include *planning techniques, estimating, social roles* and *stakeholder communications*. Projects with *strategic* intentions should include considerations for *control techniques, estimating, leadership, social roles,* and *stakeholder communications*. Projects with *cultural* intentions should have considerations for *leadership, motivation, social roles*, and *stakeholder communications* (see Table 13.5).

Table 13.5 shows the four *intentions* and which of the twelve secondary parameters ought to be considered relevant given a certain *intention*. In each of the applications of a primary parameter against all twelve secondary parameters the tables identify which of the secondaries are most relevant. An eight vote rule was used so that no primary parameter could elect more than eight secondaries (the votes may seem arbitrary but the overall rationale will be covered in chapter 14).

Parametric Algebra

Primary Parameters = <INT, BAS, ORC, PTY …>
(always "in play")

Secondary Parameters

PM   = <AUT, PRO, ORS, TEM, PLT, CTT, EST, LDR, MOT, SOR, STA, ASP>
PM | Experimental = <AUT, PRO, ~~ORS~~, TEM, ~~PLT~~, ~~CTT~~, ~~EST~~, ~~LDR~~, ~~MOT~~, SOR, ~~STA~~, ASP>
PM | Process   = <AUT, PRO, ~~ORS~~, TEM, PLT, ~~CTT~~, EST, LDR, ~~MOT~~, ~~SOR~~, ~~STA~~, ASP>
PM | Strategic   = <AUT, PRO, ~~ORS~~, ~~TEM~~, ~~PLT~~, CTT, ~~EST~~, LDR, ~~MOT~~, SOR, STA, ASP>
PM | Cultural   = <AUT, PRO, ~~ORS~~, TEM, ~~PLT~~, ~~CTT~~, ~~EST~~, LDR, MOT, SOR, STA, ~~ASP~~>

Parametric Cell Analysis

	Parameter	Intentions			
		Experimental	**Process**	**Strategic**	**Cultural**
1	Authority	√	√	√	√
2	Problem Orientation	√	√	√	√
3	Organizational Styles				
4	Teams	√	√		√
5	Planning Techniques		√		
6	Control Techniques			√	
7	Estimating		√	√	
8	Leadership		√	√	√
9	Motivation				√
10	Social Roles		√	√	√
11	Stakeholder Communications			√	√
12	Change Assumptions	√	√	√	√

Intentions Parametric Analysis
Table 13.5

Basics Assessment

Basics of a project are the commonly accepted ingredients that make the effort a project (see chapter 2). Without one or more of these *basics* the whole notion of managing the effort as a project should come under scrutiny. Many organizations require efforts to be managed as projects even if they are actually not projects. These could include the "open project" where there is no end, the leaderless project where the effort is supposed to be so clear that no one is responsible to lead it, or the project that exists independent of all others (while these others are potentially vying for the same limited resources). Missing one or more of the basic ingredients of a project brings certain secondary parameters "in play". These are highlighted in Table 13.6 in the same fashion as in the previous table.

Parametric Algebra

Primary Parameters = <INT, BAS, ORC, PTY ...>   (always "in play")

Secondary Parameters (missing)

PM	= <AUT, PRO, ORS, TEM, PLT, CTT, EST, LDR, MOT, SOR, STA, ASP>
PM | No Beginning	= <~~AUT~~, PRO, ~~ORS~~, ~~TEM~~, PLT, CTT, EST, ~~LDR~~, ~~MOT~~, ~~SOR~~, ~~STA~~, ~~ASP~~>
PM | No End	= <~~AUT~~, PRO, ~~ORS~~, ~~TEM~~, PLT, CTT, EST, ~~LDR~~, ~~MOT~~, ~~SOR~~, ~~STA~~, ~~ASP~~>
PM |No Objective	= <~~AUT~~, PRO, ~~ORS~~, ~~TEM~~, PLT, CTT, ~~EST~~, ~~LDR~~, ~~MOT~~, ~~SOR~~, ~~STA~~, ~~ASP~~>
PM | No Leader	= <AUT, PRO, ~~ORS~~, TEM, ~~PLT~~, ~~CTT~~, ~~EST~~, ~~LDR~~, ~~MOT~~, SOR, ~~STA~~, ASP>
PM | No Staff	= <AUT, ~~PRO~~, ~~ORS~~, TEM, ~~PLT~~, ~~CTT~~, ~~EST~~, LDR, MOT, ~~SOR~~, STA, ASP>
PM | No Resources	= <~~AUT~~, ~~PRO~~, ~~ORS~~, ~~TEM~~, PLT, CTT, EST, ~~LDR~~, ~~MOT~~, ~~SOR~~, STA, ~~ASP~~>
PM | No Quantitative	= <~~AUT~~, ~~PRO~~, ~~ORS~~, ~~TEM~~, PLT, CTT, EST, ~~LDR~~, ~~MOT~~, ~~SOR~~, ~~STA~~, ~~ASP~~>
PM | No Research	= <AUT, PRO, ORS, TEM, ~~PLT~~, ~~CTT~~, ~~EST~~, LDR, MOT, SOR, ~~STA~~, ~~ASP~~>
PM | No Other projects	= <AUT, PRO, ORS, TEM, ~~PLT~~, ~~CTT~~, ~~EST~~, ~~LDR~~, ~~MOT~~, ~~SOR~~, STA, ASP>

Parametric Cell Analysis

	Parameter	Beginning	End	Objective	Leader	Staff	Resources	Quant.	Research	Other Projects
		Basics								
1	Authority				√	√			√	√
2	Problem Orientation	√	√	√					√	√
3	Organizational Styles								√	√
4	Teams				√	√			√	√
5	Planning Techniques	√	√	√			√	√		
6	Control Techniques	√	√	√			√	√		
7	Estimating	√	√				√	√		
8	Leadership					√			√	
9	Motivation					√			√	
10	Social Roles			√	√				√	
11	Stakeholder Communications			√		√	√			√
12	Change Assumptions				√	√				√

Basics Parametric Analysis
Table 13.6

Organizational Context

The overall *organizational context* can be assessed in three ways (see chapter 3). The context parameter concerned with how decisions are made has values of: *autocratic* where decisions are made from the top-down, *democratic* where majority or consensus is sought, and *lassez-faire* where decisions seem to make themselves.

Context can be considered as a relationship between the supply and demand for enterprise products or services. A *classic* context is where demand is greater than supply, when demand is less than supply the context is *modern*, and when an enterprise is changing from one to the other we have the third category of *changing*.

The third form of *organizational context* is one based on how the enterprise is expected to function – like a machine (*mechanistic*) or an organism (*organic*).

These three contexts and their relationship to the secondary parameters are shown in Table 13.7.

Parametric Algebra

Primary Parameters = <INT, BAS, ORC, PTY ...>   (always "in play")

Secondary Parameters

PM   = <AUT, PRO, ORS, TEM, PLT, CTT, EST, LDR, MOT, SOR, STA, ASP>

PM | Autocratic   = <~~AUT~~, PRO, ~~ORS~~, TEM, PLT, CTT, ~~EST~~, LDR, ~~MOT~~, SOR, ~~STA~~, ASP>
PM | Democratic   = <...same...>
PM | Lassez-Faire = <...same...>

PM | Classic   = <AUT, ~~PRO~~, ORS, ~~TEM~~, ~~PLT~~, ~~CTT~~, ~~EST~~, LDR, ~~MOT~~, SOR, STA, ASP>
PM | Modern   = <...same...>
PM | Changing   = <...same...>

PM | Mechanistic – <AUT, ~~PRO~~, ORS, TEM, PLT, CTT, ~~EST~~, ~~LDR~~, ~~MOT~~, ~~SOR~~, ~~STA~~, ASP>
PM | Organic   = <...same...>

Parametric Cell Analysis

	Parameter	Decision Making Context			Supply Demand Relationship			Enterprise Performance	
		Autocratic	Democratic	Lassez-Faire	Classic	Modern	Changing	Mechanistic	Organic
1	Authority				√	√	√	√	√
2	Problem Orientation	√	√	√					
3	Organizational Styles	√	√	√	√	√	√	√	√
4	Teams	√	√	√				√	√
5	Planning Techniques	√	√	√				√	√
6	Control Techniques	√	√	√				√	√
7	Estimating								
8	Leadership	√	√	√	√	√	√	√	√
9	Motivation								
10	Social Roles	√	√	√	√	√	√		
11	Stakeholder Communications				√	√	√		
12	Change Assumptions	√	√	√	√	√	√	√	√

Organizational Context Parametric Analysis
Table 13.7

Project Aspects Assessment

Project aspects of size, requirements clarity (or structure), and level of technology needed are ways to initially look at a project. Eight possible types of projects can be identified with this assessment approach (see chapter 4). The relationships of these eight types to the secondary parameters are given in Table 13.8.

Parametric Algebra

Primary Parameters = <INT, BAS, ORC, PTY …>   (always "in play")

Secondary Parameters

PM	= <AUT, PRO, ORS, TEM, PLT, CTT, EST, LDR, MOT, SOR, STA, ASP>
PM | HS,LT,L (1)	= <~~AUT~~, PRO, ORS, ~~TEM~~, PLT, CTT, EST, LDR, ~~MOT~~, SOR, ~~STA~~, ASP>
PM | HS,LT,S (2)	= <~~AUT~~, PRO, ORS, TEM, PLT, CTT, ~~EST~~, ~~LDR~~, ~~MOT~~, ~~SOR~~, ~~STA~~, ~~ASP~~>
PM | HS,HT,L (3)	= <~~AUT~~, PRO, ORS, TEM, *PLT, CTT*, EST, LDR, ~~MOT~~, SOR, ~~STA~~, ~~ASP~~>
PM | HS,HT,S (4)	= <~~AUT~~, PRO, ORS, TEM, ~~PLT~~, ~~CTT~~, ~~EST~~, LDR, ~~MOT~~, ~~SOR~~, ~~STA~~, ~~ASP~~>
PM | LS,LT,L (5)	= <~~AUT~~, PRO, ORS, TEM, PLT, CTT, EST, LDR, ~~MOT~~, ~~SOR~~, STA, ASP>
PM | LS,LT,S (6)	= <~~AUT~~, PRO, ORS, TEM, PLT, CTT, ~~EST~~, ~~LDR~~, ~~MOT~~, ~~SOR~~, STA, ASP>
PM | LS,HT,L (7)	= <~~AUT~~, PRO, ORS, TEM, *PLT, CTT*, ~~EST~~, LDR, ~~MOT~~, SOR, STA, ASP>
PM | LS,HT,S (8)	= <~~AUT~~, PRO, ORS, TEM, ~~PLT~~, ~~CTT~~, ~~EST~~, LDR, ~~MOT~~, ~~SOR~~, STA, ASP>

Parametric Cell Analysis

	Parameter	Types							
		1 HS,LT,L	2 HS,LT,S	3 HS,HT,L	4 HS,HT,S	5 LS,LT,L	6 LS,LT,S	7 LS,HT,L	8 LS,HT,S
1	Authority								
2	Problem Orientation	√	√	√	√	√	√	√	√
3	Organizational Styles	√	√	√	√	√	√	√	√
4	Teams		√	√	√		√	√	√
5	Planning Techniques	√	√	Some		√	√	Some	
6	Control Techniques	√	√	Some		√	√	Some	
7	Estimating	√		√					
8	Leadership	√		√	√	√		√	√
9	Motivation								
10	Social Roles	√		√				√	
11	Stakeholder Communications					√	√	√	√
12	Change Assumptions					√	√	√	√

Project Aspects Parametric Analysis
Table 13.8

Table 13.9 is used to summarize or accumulate votes for the twelve secondary parameters from the other tables.

Parameters

```
PM | Process      = <AUT, PRO, ORS, TEM, PLT, CTT, EST, LDR, MOT, SOR, STA, ASP>
PM | No End       = <AUT, PRO, ORS, TEM, PLT, CTT, EST, LDR, MOT, SOR, STA, ASP>
PM | No Leader    = <AUT, PRO, ORS, TEM, PLT, CTT, EST, LDR, MOT, SOR, STA, ASP>
PM | Autocratic   = <AUT, PRO, ORS, TEM, PLT, CTT, EST, LDR, MOT, SOR, STA, ASP>
PM | Changing     = <AUT, PRO, ORS, TEM, PLT, CTT, EST, LDR, MOT, SOR, STA, ASP>
PM | LS,LT,L (5)  = <AUT, PRO, ORS, TEM, PLT, CTT, EST, LDR, MOT, SOR, STA, ASP>
```

	Parameter	Intentions	Basics	Context	Type	Total	Value
1	Authority						
2	Problem Orientation						
3	Organizational Styles						
4	Teams						
5	Planning Techniques						
6	Control Techniques						
7	Estimating						
8	Leadership						
9	Motivation						
10	Social Roles						
11	Stakeholder Communications						
12	Change Assumptions						

Parametric Analysis Summary
Table 13.9

Table 13.10 shows an example of a parametric analysis for a project identified as a process improvement, with no clear end nor clear leader, is in an autocratic/changing organizational context, is low structure (unclear requirements), uses novel technology, and is large.

Parameters "in play"

PM | Process   = <AUT, PRO, ~~ORS~~, TEM, PLT, ~~CTT~~, EST, LDR, ~~MOT~~, SOR, ~~STA~~, ASP>
PM | No End   = <~~AUT~~, PRO, ~~ORS~~, ~~TEM~~, PLT, CTT, EST, ~~LDR~~, ~~MOT~~, ~~SOR~~, ~~STA~~, ~~ASP~~>
PM | No Leader   = <AUT, ~~PRO~~, ~~ORS~~, TEM, ~~PLT~~, ~~CTT~~, ~~EST~~, ~~LDR~~, ~~MOT~~, SOR, ~~STA~~, ASP>
PM | Autocratic   = <~~AUT~~, PRO, ORS, TEM, PLT, CTT, ~~EST~~, LDR, ~~MOT~~, SOR, ~~STA~~, ASP>
PM | Changing   = <AUT, ~~PRO~~, ORS, ~~TEM~~, ~~PLT~~, ~~CTT~~, ~~EST~~, LDR, ~~MOT~~, SOR, STA, ASP>
PM | LS,LT,L (5) = <~~AUT~~, PRO, ORS, TEM, PLT, CTT, ~~EST~~, LDR, ~~MOT~~, SOR, STA, ASP>

	Parameter	Intentions	Basics	Context	Type	Total	Value
1	Authority	√	√	√		3	Formal Charisma
2	Problem Orientation	√	√	√√	√	4	Incremental
3	Organizational Styles			√	√	3	
4	Teams	√	√	√	√	4	Domain knowledge
5	Planning Techniques	√	√	√	Some	3+	Team interactions
6	Control Techniques		√	√	Some	2+	
7	Estimating	√	√			2	
8	Leadership	√		√√	√	4	
9	Motivation					0	
10	Social Roles	√	√	√√	√	5	Change Agent
11	Stakeholder Communications			√	√	2	
12	Change Assumptions	√	√	√√	√	5	Advocate

> The project should be managed using formal and charismatic authority through an incremental solution with a domain knowledge team employing lots of internal team interaction. A clear change agent should be appointed with the change agent takes on the project as an advocate for its objective.

Parametric Analysis Example Result
Table 13.10

Chapter 14

Building a Personal Parametric Model

Introduction

Building a personal parametric model can spur learning to a deeper level and provide more efficacy than the general model. Mastering the profession ought to be the goal of every serious project manager, and building these individual models gets the project manager down the road of mastering project management. Once the general model is well understood it can be used to build a personal model that suits the individual project manager and his/her environment. Actually, when mastering the general model a personalized model will unwittingly begin to take shape. The personal model is not a methodology for managing a project but a way to understand (think about) and manage a project in a deeper way.

Developing the personal model should begin with a serious review of the general model presented in this book, and during this review descriptive terms should be changed if there are others that communicated more clearly about your environment. For instance, you may have an approach for developing the project deliverable closely related to *monolithic* but call it *product life cycle development*. Also, within your environment there may be specific "givens" that will not change and therefore could be removed for subsequent project analysis – if all your teams are organized by *specialty* then the team parameter should be eliminated from the parametric list and used as a given, or constant, in any subsequent analysis. Specifics about project management may be stated in enterprise-specific methodologies and these should be given serious critical evaluation. Drawing on one's own personal knowledge and experience about how projects should be managed, along with personal preferences for dealing with the world in general, should become a part of developing a personal parametric model for managing projects.

Once the general model is mastered and the personal model begins to take shape the process of assessing a project will become more right-brain oriented. It will shift to a holistic understanding where gut-feel may outweigh detailed specifics, where rough-hewed ideas of a project become a smooth interpretation (Brenner, 2001; Gladwell, 2005; Pink, 2005).

Personal Parametric Model Development Process

Five reference sources can be used to develop a personal parametric model. These sources are:

1. The general parametric model presented in this book.
2. An accepted methodology or way for managing projects in your environment.
3. Personal knowledge of project management from education (classes, books, etc.).
4. Personal history/diary/log of actual projects engaged in previously.
5. Personal preferences for dealing with the world.

Along with these five sources, six action steps can be used to develop a personal parametric model. The first step is to evaluate the terms in the generic model (e.g. the term *leader-centric* used to describe a *team organization*) and see if they could be made clearer so that you could think about and communicate them more clearly. Second, the parameters and their values should be evaluated against the accepted way of managing projects in your environment (perhaps documented in a formal methodology). If every project is managed in a *monolithic* way there is little reason to consider the *problem orientation* parameter for every project. This parameter value is a given, not something that needs to be determined.

Third, some parameters should be discarded because they run contrary to your personal knowledge about project management. You may not know project participants well enough to understand their motivations so the *motivation* parameter should be eliminated. A reduced set of well understood parameters will result from these three steps.

Next, in step four, the reduced set of parameters should be expanded and refined using the acceptable approaches, personal history and knowledge of project management. Fifth, the expanded model should now be evaluated against personal preferences for dealing with the world. These include style of thinking (hemispheric specialization), preferred ways of dealing with information (information style per the MBTI®) (see appendix D), and motive preferences (general motivational dispositions). Special attention should be given to parameters that may not fit your personal preferences as revealed by hemispheric specialization, MBTI, and/or motivational tendencies (see Figure 14.1 and 14.2). In your personalized model be wary to exclude "uncomfortable" parameters.

Parameters	Assessment Devices		
	Hemispheric Specialization	MBTI®	Motivational Tendencies
Intentions	Left/Right	INTx	Ach, Pow
Basics	Left/Right	ESTx	Ach
Context	Right/Left	xNTx	Ach, Pow, Affil
Project Type	Left	xSTx	Ach
Authority	Left/Right	xNFx	Pow, Affil
Problem Orientation	Left	xSTx	Ach
Organizational Styles	Left	xNTx	Ach, Affil
Teams	Left/Right	ENFx	Affil, Pow
Planning Techniques	Left	ISTJ	Ach
Control Techniques	Left	xSTJ	Ach, Pow
Estimating	Left/Right	xSTx	Ach, Affil
Leadership	Right	xNFx	Pow, Ach, Affil
Motivation	Right	xNFx	Affil, Pow
Social Roles	Right	xNTx	Affil, Pow
Stakeholder Communications	Right	ESFx	Affil, Pow
Change Assumptions	Right	xNTx	Ach, Affil

Ach = Achievement
Pow = Power
Affil = Affiliation

Parameter Assessment for Personal Preference
Figure 14.1

I = Introversion	E = Extroversion
N = Intuitive	S = Sensing
T = Thinking	F = Feeling
J = Judging	P = Perceiving

MBTI Descriptors
Figure 14.2

For example, a self assessment may have shown you to have a left brain preference, be an intuitive-thinker (NT), and have a high need for achievement (Ach). Your assessment shows Left, NT, Ach so any parameter that opposes these preference you may dismiss without due consideration. In this specific case a complete opposite would be Right, SF, and Affil. These specific preferences are present for the *stakeholder communications* parameter, which you may then tend to dismiss or marginalize unless you are aware your preferences will tend to drive you away from realizing the parameter's importance.

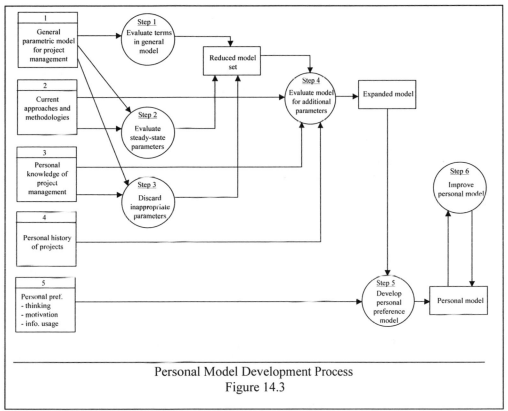

Personal Model Development Process
Figure 14.3

The sixth step uses the resultant personal parametric model to integrate continuing experiences so improvements in one's skills and abilities can lead to more experiences of success in future projects (see Figure 14.3). Continual improvement is a mastery concept (Leonard, 1992).

The best way to begin building a personal parametric model is to use a mentor or someone who knows their way around the general parametric model, and can understand you and your environment.

Projects of Life – Personal Car Cleaning

Below is an example of how to construct a set of parameters for a specific project. The example highlights how the whole notion of parametric analysis can be applied without relying on the generalized project management parametric model.

It's Saturday, the sun's shining, with a great night of rest and a pleasant breakfast of yogurt, granola, and coffee you're ready for the day. Proud of staying on your diet, the idea of getting some exercise seems in order. Cleaning the car would be perfect – it needs cleaning, and exercising outside would be nice.

All "personal car cleaning" can be described using a parametric analysis. These parameters will make up the whole concept of personal car cleaning. Each parameter has associated values that give it meaning for the project. For instance the parameter *water* could have values such as little, some, unlimited. How we go about cleaning the car will be different depending on the value of the *water* parameter – e.g. for little water we will rinse the car only once after scrubbing. By assessing these parameters one can plan the project of personal car cleaning and effectively carry it out from one time to the next even in varying situations. The parametric analysis will also help you get better each time because it contributes to more effective planning and a deeper understanding of the project – one could begin to refine the parameters and their values over time. Figure 1 below shows a parameter list and their values for this project.

Personal Car Cleaning = <Water, Weather, Equipment, Car Size, Need>

Water = <little, some, unlimited>
Weather = <clear, cloudy, storms>
Equipment = <sponge, hose, chamois>
Car Size = <large, medium, small>
Need = <low, medium, high>

Parametric Analysis for Personal Car Cleaning
Figure 1

If there's plenty of *water*, the *weather* is beautiful, we have all the necessary *equipment*, the *car size* is a medium and the *need* is high we can plan the project in terms of how much time it will take and if we have the personal energy to accomplish the task. On the other hand if there is little *water* available, the *weather* is cloudy, we only have a chamois, the *car size* is medium, and the *need* is low our cleaning will be different. We could dampen the chamois and use it alone to clean the already relatively clean car. When parameter values differ the project is different and will affect its planning, management, and execution.

This example highlights the effectiveness of the parametric analysis. This book is based on a parametric analysis of project management itself. Just as with cleaning a car, ones project management ability should improve using the parametric analysis. A deeper understanding comes from the increased ability to do more effective planning, along with a deeper understanding of the concept of project management itself.

APPENDICES

Hemispheric Dominance Inventory

Check the answers that most closely describe your preferences.

1. When discussing a movie/book, do you usually:

    A.   Relate the overall story.
    B.   Provide details of what happened.

2. Which is easiest to remember?

    A.   People's names
    B.   People's faces

3. When facing major changes in a project you usually:

    A.   Look at all the changes and address them as a whole
    B.   Evaluate each change individually and act according to each one.

4. When assembling a product (toy, appliances, etc.):

    A.   The manual is usually a last resort.
    B.   Carefully read assembly instructions before starting.

5. Which is easier to recall?

    A.   The name of a street
    B.   What the street looks like.

6. When you make decisions, do you:

    A.   Rely on your gut feeling – what feels right?
    B.   Carefully consider each option

7. When taking a test, do you prefer questions be:

    A.   Objective (multiple choice, true/false, matching)
    B.   Subjective (essay questions)

8. How are you generally considered by your coworkers?

    A.   Neat and organized
    B.   Cluttered

9.   Are you usually late for meetings or appointments?

        A.   Yes
        B.   No

10.   Do you do your best thinking:

        A.   Alone and removed from external noises.
        B.   Immersed in the activities of the project.

11.   When reading popular or trade-press material, do you:

        A.   Jump in where it seems most appealing.
        B.   Look at the table of contents, or start at the beginning of an article.

12.   When performing your job, you usually:

        A.   Concentrate on one task at a time until it is finished.
        B.   Juggle several things at once.

13.   When discussing something at work, do you:

        A.   Go straight to the overall point and then fill in the details.
        B.   Relate the details before telling where they fit in.

14.   When involved in a discussion, do you usually:

        A.   Listen very closely to what is said (the words).
        B.   Attend to how the discussion is going (tempo, volume, etc.).

15.   When speaking, do you use few or many gestures?

        A.   Use a lot of hand motions.
        B.   Use very few hand motions.

16.   When purchasing an item you really want, do you:

        A.   Save up until you can afford it.
        B.   Charge it.

17.   When expressing your opinion do you usually:

        A.   Jump right in with what is on your mind.
        B.   Think about what you are going to say first.

18.   If you were hanging something on a wall, would you:

   A.   Measure to be sure it is positioned properly.
   B.   Hang it where it looks right and move it if necessary.

19.   Do you have a well-organized office space?

   A.   Yes
   B.   No

Hemispheric Dominance Inventory – Scoring Key

Question No.	Response A	Response B
1	R	L
2	L	R
3	R	L
4	R	L
5	L	R
6	R	L
7	L	R
8	L	R
9	R	L
10	L	R
11	R	L
12	L	R
13	R	L
14	L	R
15	R	L
16	L	R
17	R	L
18	L	R
19	L	R

Motive Dispositions Questionnaire

Please rate the following items from 1 to 5 according to your agreement. Think about each item carefully and be honest with yourself.

1	2	3	4	5
Disagree	Disagree	No	Agree	Agree
Completely	Moderately	Opinion	Moderately	Completely

_____ 1. I argue with zest for my point of view against others.

_____ 2. I overcome obstacles when I try hard enough.

_____ 3. When I am with a group of people, I feel like an outsider

_____ 4. I tend to exceed the speed limit.

_____ 5. I set difficult goals for myself, which I attempt to reach.

_____ 6. I treasure my time alone and avoid too much contact with friends.

_____ 7. I can accomplish almost anything I try.

_____ 8. I enjoy organizing or directing activities of a group - team, club, or committee.

_____ 9. I like to gamble.

_____ 10. I am in my element when I am with a group of people who enjoy life.

_____ 11. Laws and rules are made simply to serve those in power.

_____ 12. I am not an organizer, and I dislike directing others.

_____ 13. Material possessions are very important to me.

_____ 14. Competition with others is something I avoid at all costs.

_____ 15. Others often seem to direct the activities of my life.

_____ 16. I don't have any close friends.

_____ 17. I am often able to solve my problems simply by asking for help from others.

_____ 18. I enjoy taking risks.

_____ 19. It is not my goal to influence other people.

_____ 20. I enjoy relaxation wholeheartedly only when it follows the successful completion of a substantial piece of work.

_____ 21. I am often forced to do what others want me to do.

_____ 22. I become very attached to my friends.

_____ 23. I have a negative self-image.

_____ 24. Rules are designed to help and protect everyone.

_____ 25. If I can't achieve something easily, I don't think it's worth it.

_____ 26. I do not like to stand out in a group

_____ 27. I always try to solve a problem myself before asking for help.

_____ 28. I like to hang around with a group of congenial people and talk about anything that comes up.

_____ 29. I feel that I change my future by what I do today.

_____ 30. I have found many things in life that I'm not good at.

_____ 31. I usually influence others more than they influence me.

_____ 32. The last thing I want is to find myself in today's competitive rat-race – like selling cars, being in business for myself, or becoming a doctor or lawyer.

_____ 33. I see myself as a loner.

_____ 34. I work like a slave at everything I undertake until I am satisfied with the result.

_____ 35. I often get to do things I want to do.

_____ 36. If people don't see my point of view, I rarely argue for it.

_____ 37. I enjoy work as much as play.

_____ 38. I feel that I can dominate a social situation.

_____ 39. I go out of my way to be with friends.

_____ 40. In general, I control the activities in my life.

_____ 41. I work hard only if it leads to pleasure and relaxation.

SCORING KEY

Instructions: Fill in the blanks below with the number that was placed next to the numbered item. Then simply sum as directed.

SELF-ATTRIBUTED ACHIEVEMENT MOTIVATION

Q#	Score	Q#	Score	
5	_____	14	_____	
20	_____	25	_____	
34	_____	32	_____	Self-Attributed Ach =
37	_____	41	_____	SumP ____ - SumN ____ + 24 = _____
SumP	_____	SumN	_____	

SELF-ATTRIBUTED AFFILIATION MOTIVATION

Q#	Score	Q#	Score	
10	_____	3	_____	
22	_____	6	_____	
28	_____	16	_____	Self-Attributed Aff=
39	_____	33	_____	SumP ____ - SumN ____ + 24 = _____
SumP	_____	SumN	_____	

SELF-ATTRIBUTED POWER MOTIVATION

Q#	Score	Q#	Score	
1	_____	12	_____	
8	_____	19	_____	
31	_____	26	_____	Self-Attributed Pow =
38	_____	36	_____	SumP ____ - SumN ____ + 24= _____
SumP	_____	SumN	_____	

SELF-ATTRIBUTED POWER BEHAVIOR

Q#	Score
4	_____
9	_____
13	_____
18	_____
23	_____
Sum	_____ = Self-attributed power behavior

SELF-ATTRIBUTED PERSONAL CAUSATION

Q#	Score	Q#	Score	
7	_____	11	_____	
24	_____	15	_____	
27	_____	17	_____	Self-Attributed PC =
35	_____	21	_____	SumP ____ - SumN ____ + 20= _____
40	_____	30	_____	
SumP	_____	SumN	_____	

Figure A-1 shows the average scores for *achievement, socialized power, affiliation*, and *personal causation* along with a band that shows plus or minus half of a standard deviation from the average. The information is based on approximately 100 scores from attendees of professional project management seminars. Most seminar attendees are professional information technologists.

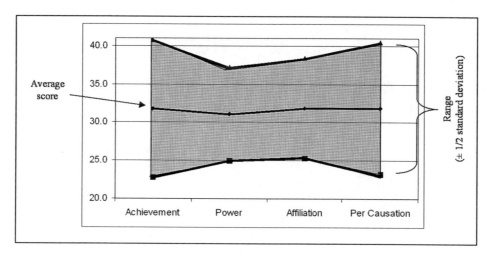

Scores from Seminar Attendees
Figure A-1

Intentions questionnaire

The following six items deal with a project's expected outcome. Each item compares one outcome against another. For each item place a single check, √, in the box that best reflects your opinion of the intention for the project. A check in "0" is appropriate if neither outcome makes sense for this project.

1.

The expected outcome is unclear

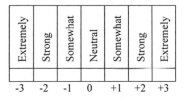

The expected outcome is to improve productivity of the enterprise

2.

Compete stronger for enterprise customers to effect the bottom line

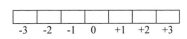

Change the assumptions people have about the enterprise

3.

Increase quality results of work tasks

Increase market penetration of end products/services

4.

Provide people a new way to value their contributions

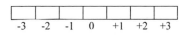

Provide a way to search for better solutions

5.

Provide or increase the standardization of processes

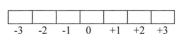

Empower people to realize their worth to the enterprise

6.

"Test the waters" to see if the kind of outcome is acceptable

Increase the positive impact of making critical business decisions.

Intentions questionnaire

The following six items deal with a project's expected outcome. Each item compares one outcome against another. For each item place a single check, √, in the box that best reflects your opinion of the intention for the project. A check in "0" is appropriate if neither outcome makes sense for this project.

	Extremely	Strong	Somewhat	Neutral	Somewhat	Strong	Extremely	

1.

| Experimental | The expected outcome is unclear | -3 -2 -1 0 +1 +2 +3 | The expected outcome is to improve productivity of the enterprise | Process |

2.

| Strategic/Eco | Compete stronger for enterprise customers to effect the bottom line | -3 -2 -1 0 +1 +2 +3 | Change the assumptions people have about the enterprise | Culture |

3.

| Process | Increase quality results of work tasks | -3 -2 -1 0 +1 +2 +3 | Increase market penetration of end products/services | Strategic/Eco |

4.

| Culture | Provide people a new way to value their contributions | -3 -2 -1 0 +1 +2 +3 | Provide a way to search for better solutions | Experimental |

5.

| Process | Provide or increase the standardization of processes | -3 -2 -1 0 +1 +2 +3 | Empower people to realize their worth to the enterprise | Culture |

6.

| Experimental | "Test the waters" to see if the kind of outcome is acceptable | -3 -2 -1 0 +1 +2 +3 | Increase the positive impact of making critical business decisions. | Strategic/Eco |

In the questionnaire each intention parameter is compared against one of the other intentions parameters. All possible comparisons are provided

Scoring of Intentions Questionnaire

Question	Experimental		Process		Strategic		Cultural	
	Score Side	Score	Score Side	Score	Score Side	Score	Score Side	Score
1	Left		Right					
2					Left		Right	
3			Left		Right			
4	Right						Left	
5			Left				Right	
6	Left				Right			
	Total Score							

Intention	Total Score	Highest Score	Number of Votes	
Experimental				
Process				
Strategic				
Cultural				

Intentions questionnaire **Example**

The following six items deal with a project's expected outcome. Each item compares one outcome against another. For each item place a single check, √, in the box that best reflects your opinion of the intention for the project. A check in "0" is appropriate if neither outcome makes sense for this project.

1.

The expected outcome is unclear

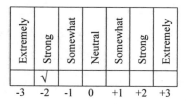

The expected outcome is to improve productivity of the enterprise

2.

Compete stronger for enterprise customers to effect the bottom line

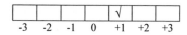

Change the assumptions people have about the enterprise

3.

Increase quality results of work tasks

Increase market penetration of end products/services

4.

Provide a way to search for better solutions

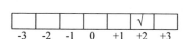

Provide people a new way to value their contributions

5.

Provide or increase the standardization of processes

Empower people to realize their worth to the enterprise

6.

"Test the waters" to see if the kind of outcome is acceptable

Increase the positive impact of making critical business decisions.

Scoring of Intentions Questionnaire

	Experimental		Process		Strategic		Cultural	
Question	Score Side	Score	Score Side	Score	Score Side	Score	Score Side	Score
1	Left	2	Right					
2					Left		Right	1
3			Left		Right	3		
4	Right						Left	2
5			Left				Right	2
6	Left	2			Right			
	Total Score	4		0		3		5

Intention	Total Score	Highest Score	Number of Votes	Overall Score
Experimental	4		1	5
Process	0		0	0
Strategic	3		1	4
Cultural	5	1	3	(9)

The Jungian theory, as employed on the Myers-Briggs Type Indicator® (MBTI®) is represented below.

Split 10 points between each of the pairs below according to your personal preference.

Worldview Focus			
	Extrovert		Introvert
	Concerned with people and things/objects in the world.		Concerned with ideas, thoughts, and/or concepts.
Points	Action oriented Outgoing Perform first, then understand Broad interests	Points	Depth in areas Inwardly focused Understand first, then act Concentration and focus

Information Gathering Focus			
	Sensing		Intuition
	Immediate facts and realities of the experience.		Possibilities, and meanings of experience.
Points	Data The facts Usability The details	Points	Possibilities Future Improvisation and hunches Meanings

Information Using Focus			
	Thinking		Feeling
	Impersonally weighing causes and outcomes.		Subjectively and personally weighing values of alternatives.
Points	Logical analysis Reasoning Rationality Explicit criteria	Points	Subjective Humane and personal Empathic Value oriented

Style of Living with Information			
	Judging		Perceiving
	Being decisive, planning and regulating events.		Being spontaneous and flexible, adapting to circumstances.
Points	Goal oriented Organizing and planning Decisive Systematic process	Points	Flexibility Emergent oriented Change is good Don't rush to decisions

Scoring Strengths

The chart below indicates strength of scoring for each two-pronged **relation** ~~~~ *extrovert* verses *introvert*). When the differences are great this **indicates a s** ~~~~ preferences for the greater of the two numbers.

Extrovert - Introvert
Sensing - Intuition
Thinking - Feeling
Judging - Perceiving

Scores	Strength
0-10	Very Strong
1-9	
2-8	Strong
3-7	
4-6	Balanced
5-5	

Your MBTI® results in one of 16 possibilities

E= Extrovert
I=Introvert

S= Sensing
N = Intuitive

T = Thinking
F = Feeling

J = Judging
P = Perceiving

A conclusion is to be able to make the following kind of statement:

"I am an *Introverted, Sensing, Thinking, Perceiving* type."

Following is the result of our image surfacing exercise. The point is to provide an overall impression of the context within which projects will need to be accomplished. The identified items are a partial representation of the "rules" of the game. There are three sections:

Section I   - An elucidation of the details of the images.
Section II - A summary of the images and key items.
Section III - General statement about the items surfaced.

Section I

Facts	Implied	Overall Assessment
Harry Potter (books) Magic School Potion creations Classes to learn/create Scientific research Make things better Have right ingredients	Learning environment Scientists as stars Search things for good Leaders have good/great ideas	Science for good Leaders are "magic"
River (thing) Constantly flowing/changing Different products Particular products now important	Company pushed around by outside forces Gone from creativity to production	Changing Risk
Dave & Busters (place) Not fun & games Generally pleasant Employees like environment Balance between family/work Something for everyone Flexibility for people Limited funds Enjoyable Challenging	Good for family people Recharging needed Nice place Limited flexibility Research/innovation	People Flexible Changing
Field of Dreams (movie) Build it Iowa Surprised win Support unsure Risky Idealistic Emerge as leading co.	Success in spite of diversity Faith in investment	Risky Adversaries Will win
Little Red Riding Hood (story) Wolf in grandmas clothes Policy preaching Democratic but still authoritarian Push back by management	Authoritarian Tricks Controlling	Mixed communication Control
Forrest Gump (movie) Great adventure Succeed in spite of Simple things Others cheer company on	Risk Hard to see truth of situation Lucky Inherent winning ability Out on top	Win through people Risk but lucky

Facts	Implied	Overall Assessment
ER (place) Caring for each other Uphill battle Maneuver politics Help when needed	Obstacles	People helping
Genetically modified corn (thing) Not apparently different Legal trial Confusing parts of org Felt duped	Tricked Intellectual leaders	Products Tricky messages
British Code breakers Break code DNA Adversaries Competitors High goal – reduce starvation	Intense work – research Outside opposition Mission bigger than the company	High goal (world class) Idealistic pursuit Outside threats
British Empire Sun never sets on the co. Spreading gospel Productivity	Has a real message/goal Lofty	High goal
Road trip to Rt. 66 Changes will occur – long and short term Opportunity and adventure Harsh weather Dealing with groups Difficult paths and detours	Thrill Risky Meet others Choices	Changes Risks More than one way
Jack be Nimble (rhyme) Dynamic co. Quick changes Nimble	People matter Cannot continue as is	Changes Nimble
Titanic (history) Well organized Good crew Threat	Current risk Known and unknown threats	Risk Threat Good crew
Peter Pan (story) Improve world Goal of never never land Captain Hook	Idealistic Exciting Adversary Improve world	High Goal Threat Puzzle
The Game (movie) Threats Exciting Trials	Works out in end	Risk Exciting Success

Section II

Image	Risk	Change	Adversaries	High Goal/Mission	Positive outcome	People
Harry Potter			X	X	X	X
River	X	X				
Dave & Busters		X				X
Field of Dreams	X		X		X	
Little Red R.H.						X
Forrest Gump	X				X	
ER	X					X
Genetic Corn			X			X
British Code B.			X	X		
British Empire				X		
Road Trip Rt. 66	X	X				
Jack be Nimble		X				
Titanic	X		X			X
Peter Pan			X	X	X	
The Game	X	X			X	X
Total	**7**	**5**	**6**	**4**	**5**	**7**

Image	Image Theme
Harry Potter	Adventure
River	Current/Flow
Dave & Busters	Opportunity
Field of Dreams	Faith
Little Red R.H.	Adversary
Forrest Gump	Adventure
ER	Support
Genetic Corn	Masked
British Code B.	Problem
British Empire	Reach
Road Trip Rt. 66	Adventure
Jack be Nimble	Nimble
Titanic	Voyage
Peter Pan	Fun & Danger
The Game	Adventure

Section III

General description
This company provides a diversity of messages across people that many times need deciphering. There is a strong impression of outside adversaries associate with a real risk of survival and adventure. There are constantly changing targets for the business, but high confidence in meeting these targets. The overall goal of the company is much larger than any of its particular initiatives, is clearly stated, and has a humanitarian component.

Bibliography

---   (1995). "CHAOS -." www.standishgroup.com Standish Group.

Achoff, R. (1981). *Creating the Corporate Future*. New York, John Wiley publisher.

Barley, S. (1990). "The alignment of technology and structure through roles and networks." *Administrative Science Quarterly*.

Benner, P. (2001). *From novice to expert: Excellence and power in clinical nursing practice*, Prentice Hall, New Jersey.

Bloom, B. (1956). *Taxonomy of educational objectives: Handbook 1: The cognitive domain*, New York, David KcKay Co.

Boulding, K. (1956). "General system theory – the skeleton of science", *Management Science*, vol 2. no. 3.

Brokaw, T. (1998). *The Greatest Generation*. New York, Random House.

Brooks, F. (1978). *The Mythical Man-Month: Essays on Software Engineering*. Reading, MA, Addison-Wesley Publishing.

Browdy, T. (2007). *Project management mastery handbook: Lessons from the field*, Alberts-Adams LLC, St. Louis, Mo.

Burns T., S., G.M. (1961). *The Management of Innovation*. London, Tavistock.

Charan, R. (1991). "How networks reshape organizations for results." *Harvard Business Review* September/October.

Churchman, C. (1968). *The Systems Approach*. New York, Dell publishing.

Cohen, M., March, J., and Olsen, J (1972). "A garbage can model of organizational choice." , *Administrative Science Quarterly*, 17, March.

Csikszentmihalyi, M. (1990). *Flow*. New York, Harper and Row Publishers.

DeCharms, R. (1983). *Personal Causation* : The Internal Affective Determinants or Behavior. Hillsdale, N.J., Lawrence Erlebaum Associates.

Diehl, R. (2003). "An explanation of changes after implementation." D.Sc. Dissertation Washington University School of Engineering and Applied Science.

Bibliography

Delisi, P. S. (1990). "Lessons from the steel axe: Culture, technology, and organizational change." *Sloan Management Review*, Fall.

Dreyfus, S. (1982). "Formal models vs. human situational understanding: inherent limitations on the modeling of business expertise", *Office: Technology and people*.

DeMarco, T. (1987). *PeopleWare: Productive Projects and Teams*. New York, Dorset House Publishing Co.

Evans, P and Wurster, T. (1997). "Strategy and the new economics of information", *Harvard Business Review*, Sept-Oct.

Ferratt, T., and Short, L. (1986). "Are information systems people different: An investigation of motivational differences." *Management Information Systems Quarterly*, December.

Fiske, F. a. T., S. (1984). *Social Cognition*. Reading, Mass, Addison-Wesley publishing.

Gladwell, M (2005). *Blink*, Back bay books, Little, Brown & Co., NY.

Goffman, E. (1959). *The Presentation of Self in Everyday Life*. New York, Doubleday, Dell Publishing Group.

Goldratt, E. (1997). *Critical Chain*. Great Barrington, MA: North River Press.

Goleman, D. et. al. (2002). *Primal leadership: Learning to lead with emotional intelligence*, Harvard press, Boston Mass.

Hammer, M. (1990). "Reengineering work: Don't automate, obliterate." *Harvard Business Review* July/August.

Harrison, A., Bramson, R. (1982). *The Art of Thinking*. New York, The Berkley Publishing Group.

Hersey, P., and Blanchard, K. (1988). *Management of Organizational Behavior: Utilizing Human Resources*. Englewood Cliffs, N.J., Prentice-Hall.

Hollander, E.P., and Julian, J.W. (1970) "Studies in Leader Legitimacy, Influence and Innovation," *Advances in Experimental Psychology* (5).

Janis, I. (1982). *Groupthink : Psychological Studies of Policy Decisions and Fiascoes*. Boston, Houghton Mifflin.

Katzenbach, J. and Smith, D. (1994). *The Disciple of Teams: Innovative Project Teams*.

Bibliography

Kidder, T. (1981). *The Soul of a New Machine*. Boston, MA, Atlantic- Little, Brown.

Kotter, J. (2001). "What leaders really do." *Harvard Business Review,* December.

Lebo, H. (1997). *The Godfather legacy: The Untold Story,*. New York, Simon & Schuster.

Lefton, R. E., Buzzotta V. R. (2000). *Leadership Through People Skills*. St. Louis, Psychological Associates.

Leonard, G. (1992). *Mastery: The keys to success and long-term fulfillment*, Plume book, Penguin Group, NY.

Locke, E., et. al. (1981). "Goal setting and task performance: 1969-1980." *Psychological Bulletin*.

Lovallo and Kahneman, D. (2003). "Delusions of success: How optimism undermines executives' decisions." *Harvard Business Review,* July.

Markus, L., Benjamin, R. (1993). "The magic bullet theory in IT-enabled transformation." *Sloan Management Review,* Winter.

McClelland, D. (1985). *Human Motivation*. Glenview, IL, Scott Foresman and Co.

McFarlan, W. (1981). "Portfolio Approach to Information Systems." *Harvard Business Review*, September.

Miller, G. A. (1956). "The magic number seven plus or minus two: Some limits on our capacity to process information." *Psychological Review,* 63.

Mills, H. (1983). *Software Productivity*. Boston, Little, Brown.

Mills, R. (1962). "How to plan and control with PERT." *Harvard Business Review,* March/April.

Mintzberg, H. (1976). "Planning on the left side and managing on the right." *Harvard Business Review,* May.

Morgan, G. (1986). *Images of Organization*. Newbury Park, CA, Sage Publications.

Myers-Briggs, I. (1980). *Gifts Differing*. Palo Alto, CA, Consulting Psychologists Press, Inc.

Bibliography

Nisbett, R., and Wilson, T. (1977). "Telling more than we know: Verbal reports on mental processes." *Psychological Review,* 84.

Orlikowski, W. (1996). "Improvising organizational transformation over time: A situated change perspective." *Information Systems Research,* 7, March.

Ossorio, P (1981). "Conceptual notational devices: The PCF and related types", *Advances in descriptive psychology,* vol. 1, ed. K. Davis

Ossorio, P (1981). "Explanation, falsifiability, and rule-following," in *Advances in descriptive psychology,* vol. 1. , ed. K. Davis

Ossorio, P. (1983). "A multicultural psychology." *Advances in Descriptive Psychology* , Davis, K. and Berger, R. (Eds.).

Perkins, D. (2000). *Leading At The Edge: Leadership lessons from the extraordinary saga of Shackleton's Antarctic expedition.* New York, AMACOM.

Pinder, C. (1984). *Work Motivation: Theory, Issues, and Applications.* Glenview, IL, Scott, Foresman and Co.

Pink, D. H. (2005). A Whole New Mind: Why Right-Brainers will Rule the Future, Riverhead books, NY.

Porter, M. a. M., V. (1985). "How information gives you competitive advantage." *Harvard Business Review,* July/August.

Putman, A. (1988). "Organizations." *Advances in Descriptive Psychology,* K. Davis and A. Putman (Eds.).

Rogers, E. (1995). *Diffusion of Innovations.* New York, The Free Press.

Schein, E. H. (1985). *Organizational Culture and Leadership: A Dynamic View.* San Francisco, Jossey-Bass.

Schon, D. (1987). *Educating the reflective practitioner.* Jossey-Bass publishers, San Francisco, CA.

Senge, P. (1990). *The Fifth Discipline: The Practice of the Learning Organization.* New York, Doubleday.

Siehl, C. (1985). "After the founder", in *Organizational Culture (Frost, P. et al eds.),* Sage publications, Beverly Hills, CA.

Bibliography

Simon, II. A. (1977). *The New Science of Management Decision*, Englewood Cliffs, N.J., Prentice-Hall.

Slovic, P., Fishhoff, B. , Lichtenstein S. (1982). "Facts versus fears: Understanding perceived risk", *Judgment Under Uncertainty: Heuristics and Biases*. D. Kahneman (Ed.). New York, Cambridge University Press.

Snyder, M. (1987). Public *Appearances Private Realities: The psychology of self-monitoring*, NY, Freeman press.

Stair, R. a. R., G. (1999). *Principles of Information Systems*. New York, Course Technology.

Stanislavski, C. (1936). *The Actor Prepares*. New York, Routledge.

Strauss, A., Corbin, J. (1990). *Basics of Qualitative Research: Grounded Theory Procedures and Techniques*. Newbury Park, CA, Sage Publications.

Tuckman, Bruce W., and Mary-Ann C. J. (1977). "Stages of small-group development revisited", *Group & Organization Studies* Vol 2 (No. 4).

Tversky, A., Kahneman, D. (1974). "Judgment under uncertainty: Heuristics and biases." *Science*, 185.

Tversky, A., Kahneman, D. (1981). "The framing of decisions and the psychology of choice." *Science*, 211.

von Bertalanffy, L. (1951). "General systems theory: A new approach to unity of science, *Human Biology*, vol 23.

Weick, K. (1979). *The Social Psychology of Organizing*. Reading, MA, Addison-Wesley publishing.

Weinberg, G. M. (1971). *The Psychology of Computer Programming*. New York, Van Nostrand Reinhold.

Wenger, E. (2006). *Communities of practice: Learning, meaning, and identity*, Cambridge University press, Cambridge.

Wiest, J., Levy, F. (1977). *A Management Guide to PERT/CPM with GERT/PDM/DCPM and Other Networks*. Englewood Cliff, NJ, Prentice-Hall Inc.

Bibliography

Yourdon, E. a. C., L. (1979). *Structured Design: Fundamentals of a Discipline of Computer Program and System Design*. Englewood Cliffs, N.J., Prentice-Hall.

Zientara, M. (1981). *The history of computing*, Computerworld comm., Mass.

Bibliography

Additional References

Block, R. (1983). *The Politics of Projects*. New York, Yourdon Press.

Burrill, C. and Ellsworth., L. (1980). *Modern Project Management*. Tenafly, N.J., BEA, Inc.

DeMarco, T. (1982). *Controlling Software Projects*. New York, Yourdon Press.

DeMarco, T. and. Lister, T. (1987). *Peopleware: Productive Projects and Teams*. New York, Dorset House Publishing.

Frame, D. (1995). *Managing Projects in Organizations: How to Make the Best Use of Time, Techniques, and People*. San Francisco, Jossey-Bass Publishers.

Project Management Institute. (2008). *A Guide to the Project Management Body of Knowledge (PMBOK Guide) –2000 Edition*, Project Management Institute.

Kerzner, H. (2005). *Project Management: A Systems Approach to Planning, Scheduling, and Controlling*. New York, John Wiley & Sons, Inc.

Kerzner, H. (2004). Advance *Project Management: Best practices on implementation*. New York, John Wiley & Sons, Inc.

Metzger, P. (1981). *Managing a Programming Project*. Englewood Cliffs, N.J., Prentice-Hall, Inc.

Rakos, J. (1990). *Software Project Management for Small to Medium Size Projects*. Englewood Cliffs, N.J., Prentice-Hall, Inc.

Schwalbe, K. (2008). *Information Technology Project Management*. Canada, Course Technology - Thomson.

Shtub A., B., J., and Globerson, S. (1994). Pro*ject Management: Engineering, Technology, and Implementation*. Englewood Cliffs, N.J., Prentice-Hall, Inc.

Thomsett, R. (1980). *People and Project Management*. New York, Yourdon Press.

Wysocki, R., Beck, R., Crane, D. (2007). Effec*tive Project Management: Traditional, Adaptive, Extreme*. New York, John Wiley and Sons, Inc.

Index

Index

Index

Index